Waltham F⸱ ⸱es

Please return this item by ⸱'
renewed unl⸱

D0719525

The Lunatics
Have Taken Over
The Asylum

The Lunatics Have Taken Over The Asylum

POLITICAL LETTERS
TO
The Daily Telegraph

EDITED BY IAIN HOLLINGSHEAD

Constable • London

CONSTABLE

First published in Great Britain in 2015 by Constable

A CIP catalogue record for this book
is available from the British Library.

ISBN 978-1-47212-154-7 (hardback)
ISBN: 978-1-47212-155-4 (ebook)

1 3 5 7 9 10 8 6 4 2

Typeset in Great Britain by SX Composing DTP, Rayleigh, Essex
Printed and bound in Great Britain by Clays Ltd, St Ives plc

Constable
is an imprint of
Constable & Robinson Ltd
Carmelite House
50 Victoria Embankment
London EC4Y 0DZ

An Hachette UK Company
www.hachette.co.uk

www.littlebrown.com

SIR — There is no doubt that the population of Britain includes very many intelligent and honest men and women. Why do so few of them become politicians?

James Farquhar
Girvan, Ayrshire

Contents

Introduction

Telegraph letter writers are probably not alone in thinking that politics has taken some strange turns in recent years. Thanks to the first coalition government since 1945 we know more than we used to — perhaps an awful lot more than we need to — about Chris Huhne's driving, Andrew Mitchell's vocabulary, James Murdoch's memory, Rebekah Brooks's horses, Boris Johnson's water cannons, the Queen's purring, Greggs' pasties, Jimmy Carr's tax returns, Nigel Farage's drinking, the Bullingdon Club's rituals and the ins and outs of same-sex marriage. And yet the long-suffering electorate still has absolutely no idea what the 'Big Society' means. Neither, it seems, does David Cameron.

Meanwhile, the public has twice since 2010 bade an enthusiastic goodbye to Gordon Brown — only to be left with Ed Miliband, Russell Brand and Nigel Farage instead. Neither Ed Balls, nor Tony Blair, his rival for the title of 'most annoying man in politics', shows any sign of going quietly. Boris Johnson is contemplating a return to Parliament. Vince Cable is still in the Cabinet. No wonder Nick Clegg admits to enjoying a good cry. Or that David Cameron took his own advice to 'calm down, dear' and spent so much time 'chillaxing' in Cornwall, where he could forget about his 'cast-iron' promises on an EU referendum.

Five years is a long time in politics. Fortunately, it has also been a fertile period for the *Telegraph*'s legion of witty letter writers and their loyal army of fans. Notwithstanding *Private Eye*'s entertaining caricature of Sir Herbert Gussett, the ur-*Telegraph* letter writer and resident of The Old Asylum, Loonraker, Somerset, our diverse correspondents are endowed with a rare combination of mischief, erudition and robust common sense which makes them particularly astute political commentators.

Where else, except on the letters pages of the *Daily Telegraph*, could you find a diplomat who met Gaddafi during the revolution in 1969; a television producer who unsuccessfully had the frighteners put on him by Alastair Campbell; an MP who took part in the EU membership debate of 1975; and a relative of the Earl of Essex, who had his ears boxed by Queen Elizabeth I, who hopes that the present Queen will do the same to David Cameron? They are all collected together in this book, alongside a smattering of retired colonels (and squadron leaders); peers, QCs and irate citizens; Frederick Forsyth, who is rather opposed to the EU; Oleg Gordievsky, who is equally antipathetic to Vladimir Putin; a man who knocked over Harold Wilson while on holiday in the 1960s on the Isles of Scilly; a brave fellow who bumped into Denis Thatcher in the loo and suggested that his wife should resign; and someone who met Ed Balls on a train and thought he would benefit from reading the *Telegraph*.

Of course, all lawmakers should follow such wise advice and find out what the electorate is really thinking. While anyone can rant on Twitter about current affairs, only *Telegraph* letter writers would think to compare the Leveson report to John Milton's *Areopagitica*; Islamic State to Valerius Maximus; coalition disharmony to the feuding between Balfour and Bonar Law; the London riots of 2011 to the Gordon Riots of 1780; Nick Clegg's work ethic to that of Field Marshal Viscount Slim; or Plebgate to Mr Toad's fifteen-year sentence for 'cheeking the police'.

To all our wonderful letter writers, as well as to Sally Peck, Deputy Letters Editor at the Telegraph, who mined the archives with great skill, my grateful thanks for providing such a fun and wide-ranging retrospective on the Coalition government.

Whether providing serious insight into the rise of UKIP or gloriously silly analysis of George Osborne's glottal stops and David Cameron's dress sense, theirs is a welcome voice of sanity in a world in which the lunatics appear finally to have taken over the asylum.

Iain Hollingshead

1. Goodbye, Gordon

NEW YEAR'S RESOLUTIONS 2010

SIR – Dear Lord, I know I am not one with whom you speak,
but I note that you have seen fit to take away the heart-throb
actor, Patrick Swayze, the Jackson fellow with the sweet
my favourite musician, Bird. I have two small boys to bring up
on my own, Alan Beckett...

I just wanted to let you know, while you're choosing, our next
minister is Gordon Brown, sir...

I DON'T AGREE WITH...

SIR – I for one will not be swayed by a politician who empties
the electorate that he stands behind by putting his hand in
his pockets, as did Nick Clegg. Perhaps underlining the
relaxed debate. Can we know a man's motives at election?
... Male

Literature, Attitude Campaigns, Sydney French,
Pembroke Gardens, London

SIR – So this is what we know about our elected political
punditry based on the treasury's atmosphere. So what of
the choice of a prime minister with a climate in which party
faces its deepest post-war equilibrium – deciding on
whether or not someone be the leader in the process.

NEW YEAR'S RESOLUTIONS 2010

SIR – Dear Lord, I know that I don't talk to you that much, but I note that you have recently taken away my favourite actor, Patrick Swayze, my favourite actress, Farrah Fawcett, my favourite musician, Michael Jackson, and my favourite cricketer, Alec Bedser.

I just wanted to let you know that my favourite prime minister is Gordon Brown. Amen.

David Say
St Ives, Cornwall

I DON'T AGREE WITH NICK

SIR – I for one will not be voting for a man who so despises the electorate that he stands before them with his hands in his pockets, as did Nick Clegg the other night during the televised debate. Can we now expect him to address us all as *Mate*?

Lieutenant Commander Philip Barber (retd)
Norton Juxta Twycross, Leicestershire

SIR – So this is what we have come to: instant political punditry based on the tracking of a computer worm, and the choice of a prime minister – at a time when the nation faces its deepest post-war economic crisis – resting on whether or not someone has his hands in his pockets.

The final debate should include a dancing dog and a bird impressionist. Who knows – the dog could take the lead, or the bird man may get the worm.

Michael Cassell
St Raphael, Var, France

SIR – The national debt is increasing at about £6,000 per second. I couldn't help but think it should have been displayed, whirling away, at the bottom of the television screen as the three party leaders reeled off their spending commitments.

Dr A. Dyson
Southwell, Nottinghamshire

SIR – Let us not forget that this is how the United States got George W. Bush – twice.

Roger Moore
Westbury-on-Severn, Gloucestershire

SIR – If a week is a long time in politics, then ninety minutes is a close second.

Anthony Lord
Thornton-Cleveleys, Lancashire

SIR — 'The great thing in life, Jeeves, if we wish to be happy and prosperous, is to miss as many political debates as possible' (*Much Obliged, Jeeves*).

Stephen Farrow
London SE3

SIR — The television debate reminded me of a high-school exercise, with Gordon Brown as the dour headmaster, David Cameron as the politics master and Nick Clegg as the precocious sixth-former trying to impress his mates.

Elizabeth Luders
Knebworth, Hertfordshire

SIR — Mr Clegg's performance was like the best man making the best speech at a wedding reception. He gets laughs and applause, but he isn't getting married.

Mike Phelps
Yeovil, Somerset

SIR — Why all the fuss about Nick Clegg's performance? By his own admission he managed to sweet-talk at least thirty women into his bed.

Sandra Mitchell
London W13

SIR – What will be the response of the many voters who fail to find the name Clegg on their ballot papers on 6 May?

David Coulston
Longridge, Lancashire

SIR – Cleggs are what we call horseflies in Scotland. I was bitten by one when on holiday in Europe, appropriately enough, and it drew blood. It circled me for a second bite, but I flattened it before it could do so. The bite was, of course, a dirty one and took some time to heal up.

A. H. N. Gray
Edinburgh

SIR – The most astonishing fact is that Gordon Brown finished third out of three and his acolytes are relieved. I dread their ambitions for the country.

Kiran Solanki
Oadby, Leicestershire

SIR – I had expected to enjoy heartily the spectacle of the Prime Minister clumsily attempting to present himself as a normal, contented, media-friendly human being.

However, the effect of his combined humiliations this week is akin to watching a starving man trying to eat soup with a tennis racket. On humanitarian grounds, I can no longer derive pleasure from it.

This will not translate into a sympathy vote, but I wish him well in his imminent retirement.

C. Ross
Poole, Dorset

WHEN GORDON MET GILLIAN

SIR – The most damning aspect was not Gordon Brown calling Gillian Duffy a bigot, but the fact that he thought it was 'ridiculous' to be put in a position to talk to 'that woman' and be forced to hear her views.

If ever evidence was needed of this Labour government's refusal to listen to grassroots feelings on matters of concern, this incident has provided it.

Russell Armitage
Walsall, Staffordshire

SIR – I would think that Gillian Duffy, sixty-five, is probably more annoyed at being described as 'elderly' than a 'bigot'.

Andrew J. Morrison (64 yrs and 355 days)
Faveraye-Machelles, France

SIR – If I had been in Gordon Brown's shoes when leaving Gillian Duffy's house to face the media I would have hung my head in shame for what I had said, not stood there smiling like a hyena with diarrhoea.

J. R.
Scarborough, North Yorkshire

SIR – I always thought *The Thick of It* was a bit far-fetched. Not anymore.

Min Larkin
Halton, Buckinghamshire

SIR – I was hugely reassured by Gordon Brown's gaffe. He does stupid things, just like I do. It highlights the folly of spending hundreds of thousands of pounds charging around the country trying to convince the British people that in no way are you actually a complete penguin.

David S.-P.
India

SIR – As a child of the manse, Mr Brown ought to have paid more attention to the words in Luke's Gospel (12:3): 'That which ye have spoken in the ear in closets shall be proclaimed upon the housetops.'

Lindsay Allen
Carrickfergus, Co. Antrim

HOW TO CHOOSE AN MP

SIR – I knew a professor at college who had an unusual method of deciding which party would obtain his vote. He acquired copies of all the manifestos and proceeded to mark them as one would an essay. He subsequently voted for the party whose manifesto contained the fewest grammatical errors.

Harry Drummond
Midhurst, West Sussex

SIR – I will give my vote to any party that gives us back public transport on Christmas Day.

Trevor Neilsen
London W6

SIR – 'A wise man's heart inclines him toward the right, but a fool's heart toward the left' (Ecclesiastes 10:2).

Jola Glaser
London W5

SIR – After we have read the *Daily Telegraph* front to back, I use the paper to line the bottom of our parrots' four cages, with the Labour candidates face up.

Daphne MacOwan
Ramsey, Isle of Man

SIR — I wonder how many of your readers are like me in wishing the leaders of our main parties were Samantha Cameron, Sarah Brown and Miriam Clegg.

Iris J. L. Wells
York

I'M NOT FEELING LUCKY

SIR — On election day I typed into Google: 'Who is going to win . . .' The suggested options were headed by the Royal Rumble 2010, followed by *Celebrity Big Brother*, *Big Brother*, *Celebrity Big Brother* 2010 and World Cup 2010, with the general election in sixth place.

These options are based on other users' search activity.

This leaves me nearly lost for words, but my answers are, in order: What? Who cares? Who cares? Who cares? Hopefully England (but probably not) and I don't know, but fear the worst.

Trevor Mudd
Addlestone, Surrey

SIR — Unless there is a divine typographical error, David Cameron need have no fears. A leaflet from our Conservative candidate in the local elections, Chris Morrall, states: 'Christ intends to work closely with Mark Garnier, the Conservative Parliamentary candidate.'

Peter Ricketts
Kidderminster, Worcestershire

SIR – Having seen footage of the BBC election-night party on the Thames, can I assume that if I'd turned up waving my TV licence I would have been admitted?

John Wilson
Princes Risborough, Buckinghamshire

RIGHTING THE WRONGS OF A HUNG PARLIAMENT

SIR – Now that we have a hung Parliament, perhaps we should adopt the system of voting used in EU referendums, where the poll is run again and again until the 'right' result is obtained.

Colin Goodall
Hazleton, Gloucestershire

SIR – I note that all three major party leaders say that what we need now is a government that will govern in the 'national interest', almost as though this is a novel concept.

Who else's interest would they govern for? Not their own, surely?

Richard Longthorp
Howden, East Yorkshire

SIR – I look forward to all those Liberal Democrats elected with less than 50 per cent of the vote resigning on the basis that the votes against them were proportionally greater.

Colin H. Bond
Vale, Guernsey

SIR – I see that David Barnes, the Independent English Delegate candidate for the Hertford and Stortford seat, polled no votes.

Truly independent, he appears not to have voted for himself.

Richard Nash
London E1

I CAN SEE CLEARLY NOW GORDON HAS GONE

SIR – A small crowd of us gathered at the gates of Buckingham Palace to witness the handover of power. The change in the weather provided the biggest amusement.

When Gordon Brown was seeing the Queen, the sky was dark and brooding. After he left, and as David Cameron made his way to the palace, the sky began to clear in the distance, and a large rainbow appeared over Whitehall.

By the time Cameron left, the sky was almost completely blue.

John Shields
London SW1

SIR — I noticed that Gordon Brown took very slow steps back into Downing Street after making his final statement as prime minister. I wasn't sure whether he looked more like an undertaker walking in front of a hearse or someone suffering an acute attack of piles.

It would be wonderful if it could be arranged for a gospel choir to be positioned outside when he leaves office to sing 'Oh Happy Day'.

Richard Martin
Epsom, Surrey

SIR — All that dreadful and, presumably, expensive cosmetic dentistry for nothing.

Colin Forsyth
Uppingham, Rutland

SIR — I am taking a prime ministerial and statesman-like decision to resign from my tennis club, because I cannot win.

Jeff Wilcox-Smith
Wing, Leicestershire

SIR — Has Gordon Brown been running Rangers FC since he ceased to be prime minister?

Jon Redfern
Cleobury Mortimer, Shropshire

SIR — I read that Gordon Brown has been appointed United Nations Special Envoy for Global Education. Can this be the same Gordon Brown who spoke of 'one pence' in a budget speech as Chancellor?

Geoffrey Hodgson
Shadwell, West Yorkshire

SIR — What a relief not to have numerous Scottish accents telling us what to do.

John Reeves
Fairseat, Kent

SIR — It was nice of Mr Brown to wait until after *The Archers* to announce his resignation. Sadly, the new worries that cloud my head — Pip and Jude, on or off; Helen, with or without child — make recent political events seem straightforward.

Patrick Finn
Hornsea, East Yorkshire

SIR — I must stop rushing to turn off the radio when I hear the phrase, 'The Prime Minister said'.

N. P. Scott
Harpenden, Hertfordshire

PROPHETIC CROSS WORDS

SIR – On election day, I bought in a charity shop a virgin *Daily Telegraph Crossword Diary* for 2006. One of the first clues I tried was: 'What the Conservatives and the Liberals do not do [5].'

The answer? 'Agree.'

Ken Wortelhock
Devonport, New Zealand

SIR – Now that a historic deal has been concluded between the Tories and the Lib Dems, memories of the 1931 National government have come flooding back to me.

Within months, the Liberal Party split in half and the followers of Sir John Simon remained on the government benches, and those of Sir Herbert Samuel crossed the floor and sat on the Opposition benches. Sir John Simon and his followers became National Liberals. Coalition has bitter memories for Liberals, and could well split the party once again.

Terry Farmer
Sherborne, Dorset

SIR – Fifty-seven seats, a net loss of five seats, leading to five Cabinet positions including a deputy prime minister. Talk about disproportional representation.

Daniel Jeory
Chester

SIR — The Conservative-Lib Dem coalition is welcome because it marks a victory for eighteenth- and nineteenth-century classical-liberal ideas — developed by thinkers such as David Hume, Adam Smith and John Stuart Mill — over the discredited Big Government twentieth-century version of liberalism, supported by philosophers such as John Rawls.

Many of us who believe in the right of individuals to control their lives have found themselves backing the free-market stance of the Tories, while preferring the more robust support for civil liberties promoted by the Liberal Democrats.

The creation of a government that supports liberal conservatism is a significant and welcome realignment in our politics, which could eventually lead to a full merger between the two parties in coalition.

Maurice Taylor
Bristol

SIR — Two public-school, Oxbridge, white males running the country. New politics?

James Conboy
Liverpool

SIR – In Michael Portillo's eager expectation of the demise of his old foe the 'Tory Party Right' he forgets his history. This is particularly regrettable in an erstwhile pupil of that sage of the Tory Right, Maurice Cowling, whose work on Disraeli's 1867 Reform Act shows the pitfalls for Conservative leaders who forsake their supporters in pursuit of a Liberal coalition. By proposing electoral reform, Disraeli alienated his backbenchers, putting himself at the mercy of the Liberal Party. The result: Disraeli's attempts at moderate reform were washed away in a flood of radical amendments, and the Tories went down to a landslide election defeat the following year.

James Kirby
Balliol College, Oxford

THE ROSY GARDEN

SIR – Am I alone in thinking that Nick and Dave were going to walk away from their first press conference in the Downing Street Rose Garden holding hands?

John Ward
Ashampstead, Berkshire

SIR – After David killed Goliath (Gordon Brown), Jonathan (Nick Clegg) 'loved him as his own soul' and 'stripped himself of the [political] robe that was upon him, and gave it to David'.

Then, when Saul (Lib Dem rebels) determined to slay David, Jonathan departed from him for ever. 'They kissed one another, and wept one with another.'

But it was Jonathan who perished. 'I am distressed for thee, my brother Jonathan,' David lamented. 'Thy love to me was wonderful, passing the love of women. How are the mighty fallen.'

How long until this tale comes true?

John Fordham
London NW1

SIR — I was always told to check a candidate's shoes as he entered the interview room. The poor condition of both pairs of shoes in the Downing Street garden told us everything we need to know about them.

Sean Hayward
Marple Bridge, Cheshire

SIR — Nick Clegg has a very similar appearance and bearing to the Prime Minister, and I have noticed that he is now beginning to sound like him.

Is this a development of the Crufts syndrome, whereby master and dog begin to look alike? If so, which one's the master?

Malcolm Allen
Berkhamsted, Hertfordshire

SIR – Are David Cameron and Nick Clegg morphing into Ant and Dec?

Henry Page
Newhaven, East Sussex

SIR – Perhaps it is now time for the Conservative (tree) and the Liberal (bird) emblems to link up. Surely the bird could be neatly perched on one of the lower branches?

Andrew Cooper
London N11

SIR – Andrew Cooper's suggestion is excellent, provided the electorate is not, eventually, covered by what is usually found beneath trees with birds perched in the lower branches.

Owen Hay
Colchester, Essex

SIR – Having heard the word progressive more often in the past ten days than in any time during my lifetime, I decided to look the word up in my dictionary.

Progressive: proceeding gradually in stages; a progressive decline in popularity; (of a disease or ailment) increasing in severity: (of tax) increasing as a proportion of the sum taxed as that sum increases.

Now everything is clear.

Fenella Ignatiev
Deal, Kent

2. Hello, Austerity

GROSS DOMESTIC UNHAPPINESS

SIR – Does the old saying 'we were poor, but we were happy' indicate that the government is less than confident of our economic well-being in the future, and needs a poorness/happiness index?

Michael McVeigh
Helensburgh, Dunbartonshire

SIR – Well-being is one thing; happiness is quite another. No one who thinks is happy.

Mary Fudge
Watford, Hertfordshire

CUTTING THE CORDUROY DEFICIT

SIR – As David Cameron struggles to save money, he could well look at Sport, Culture, Art and Music (SCAM), which have drained the British taxpayer of some £560 million every year for the last twenty years, to the benefit of no one except the thousands of luvvies that this money keeps in fine corduroy style.

Surely they could do just as well down a coal mine, if only to marvel at the wonder of it all.

Malcolm Parkin
Kinnesswood, Kinross

SIR – Mr Cameron should follow Churchill's example. In the early 1950s, when announcing harsh measures, he ordered a 15 per cent cut in salaries for his Cabinet, as opposed to the cut in income tax, which many of Mr Cameron's colleagues will be enjoying today.

Many of the cuts in handouts are necessary, but ministers announcing them should appear human.

Charles Simeons
Cley, Norfolk

SIR – Following a governmental purge in the 1970s, I remember publication, by the Civil Service College, of the book *Public Expenditure Management and Control*.

Our small, but zealous, office library instantly ordered seven copies.

James Algar
Hockley, Essex

SIR – 'The Civil Service,' said the late Dr Piet Koornhof, a South African nationalist Cabinet minister, is 'like a tortoise. It goes slowly about its business, but pick it up or touch it and it stops altogether.'

Michael Brown
Hilton, KwaZulu-Natal, South Africa

SIR – Leaving my Civil Service office one evening, I passed a colleague sitting at his desk staring into space. I suggested that he went home. He replied that he could not as he wanted a 'flexi' day off next week and needed to build up some more time.

Ted Shorter
Tonbridge, Kent

SIR – The British Embassy in Bangkok is advertising in the local press for a climate change officer, which involves working with colleagues in other British embassies in south-east Asia, and reporting to a team leader based in Singapore.

It is comforting to know that such vital positions have escaped the spending cuts.

John Prior
Bangkok

SIR – If we charged for all the terrorist training carried out in Britain it could relieve the country of its debt within a year or so.

A. P.
Warwick

SIR – The national debt could be cleared in a week if a £100 fixed penalty was applied to anyone parking on the pavement.

Jim Alexander
Lichfield, Staffordshire

SIR – Would it not be much simpler if Whitehall took all our money and gave us weekly pocket-money?

Eric Howarth
Bourne, Lincolnshire

SIR – My wife says there was a recipe for bread soup in your *Weekend* section. I knew the economy wasn't in the best shape, but it's not that bad, surely?

T. H.
Hawkinge, Kent

SIR – Walking through the ancient streets of Shrewsbury last night I was assailed by one of the many people apparently down on his luck and begging for money. I decided to ignore him as he was making a call on his pristine iPhone 4.

John D. Neal
Shrewsbury

SIR – You report that arrests have been made in connection with the discovery of four million counterfeit pound coins. Far from being charged, surely these enterprising individuals should be rewarded for their entrepreneurial flair? After all, they are only assisting the Bank of England with its programme of quantitative easing, while relieving the taxpayer of the minting costs.

Alan Duncalf
Bampton, Devon

SIR – Before cutting back on security, David Cameron should heed the fate of Olof Palme. The late Swedish Prime Minister refused all security and was assassinated walking home.

In such circumstances, Nick Clegg would become prime minister. It's a cut too far.

Brian Clivaz
London SW9

SIR – I have to admit that I misjudged the strength of feeling by public-sector workers against the cuts – right up to the moment I tried to reduce by 25 per cent the amount of housekeeping money I give to my wife.

Hugh Stewart-Smith
London E11

THE BENEFITS OF A
SMALL SOCIETY

SIR – I aspire to provide a caring home for my family and to be there for my children outside school hours. As a stay-at-home mum, I volunteer at my children's school, have been the treasurer of its parent-teacher association and am currently chairman of the parish council. My salary? A pay cut by the removal of child benefit. So much for the Big Society.

Sarah Powell
Somerford Keynes, Gloucestershire

SIR – Why stop child benefit at eighteen? I have three children ranging from twenty-six to thirty-nine and I am more in need of child allowance than ever.

Jeremy Lane
Bampton, Oxfordshire

SIR – So women who go out to work are to get help with the cost of child care, because they are prepared to 'work hard'.

Is David Cameron really saying that a woman who stays at home to look after the children she has brought into this world, cooking, cleaning, washing, ironing, shopping and possibly gardening, seven days a week, fifty-two weeks a year, is not working hard? Oh foolish, foolish man, you should try it!

Lady Smith

Marlow Common, Buckinghamshire

SIR – Have I got this right? David Cameron's 'moral mission' is based on the idea that the only way to motivate poor people is to give them less money and the only way to motivate rich people is to give them more money.

Nigel Pedley

Matlock, Derbyshire

SIR – £150 a year as a tax benefit for married couples is about 40p a day.

It reminds me of the old saying (when 7s 6d was the price of a marriage licence): 'Seven and six, was she worth it?'

Mike Bridgeman

Market Lavington, Wiltshire

SIR – The Big Society is here now. I saw some of its representatives waddling out of a fast-food shop today.

Malcolm Allen

Berkhamsted, Hertfordshire

SIR — Recently I happened to be in a court building and noticed that someone had spilt a cup of coffee down the main stairway.

On pointing it out to an attendant I was jokingly asked if I would like to get a mop. On my return that afternoon, I noticed two large yellow cones on the stairs warning that there was a slippery surface.

The following morning they were still there, with the dried coffee.

It would have taken precisely the same amount of time to get a wet cloth and wipe up the coffee as it did to position the cones.

Until this jobsworth attitude to life changes, you can forget the Big Society.

Angela Symondson
Bledlow, Buckinghamshire

SIR — There is no such thing as Big Society.

Andrew Casey
Epsom, Surrey

SIR — Will the government be communicating with us through the *Big Issue*?

Peter J. L. de Snoo
Perranwell, Cornwall

SIR — On Wednesday we took our grandchildren on a train trip to Shepreth Wildlife Park. We miscounted the number of stops and mistakenly got off the train at Meldreth, where we had to wait an hour for the next train.

The station supervisor provided us with a kettle of hot water, coffee, tea, milk and sugar. The station itself had a tidy garden provided by the gardening club of a local primary school.

Is this an example of the Big Society in action? We'd like to thank everyone.

Frank Waters
Letchworth, Hertfordshire

THE SQUEEZED MIDDLE

SIR — Am I alone in speculating that the Chancellor of the Exchequer has mislaid his belt while expecting us to tighten ours?

One has only to compare the squeezed cut of his jacket, which appears to show his trousers falling down, with the proportionate elegance displayed by the Duke of Edinburgh.

Patrick Williams
Canterbury, Kent

SIR – I do wish politicians would stop wearing make-up. In your front-page photograph of George Osborne he looks like a pantomime dame.

Raymon Doyle
Bearwood, Dorset

SIR – While I am generally in favour of people learning on the job, I think it mindless to entrust the post of Chancellor of the Exchequer to George Osborne, whose sole qualification for the role appears to be his boundless self-confidence.

Andy Smith
Kingston-upon-Thames, Surrey

SIR – Is it not very peculiar of the Prime Minister to make a speech only thirteen days before the Budget telling us what the Chancellor is not going to do? Why keep a Chancellor and bark yourself?

I suppose it is better than the position when Tony Blair was Prime Minister and Gordon Brown refused to tell him what was going to be in the Budget.

But for whom was the speech made – investors, Tory voters or the malcontents on the Tory backbenches? It certainly didn't cheer me up.

Richard Johnson
London SW6

SIR – Last week I thought that the petrol tank in my car was half full. Now I realize to my horror that it is actually half empty.

Bob Bruford
Horsham, West Sussex

JIMMY DODGERS

SIR – David Cameron was not wrong to attack Jimmy Carr over his tax avoidance. In the Second World War they attacked war profiteers. Now we have tax profiteers who pay less than their share towards the costs of the police or National Health Service.

Paul Brazier
Wotton-under-Edge, Gloucestershire

SIR – To be taken seriously both comedians and politicians need to be squeaky clean.

Stephen Gledhill
Evesham, Worcestershire

SIR – I put my savings into a tax-avoidance scheme. It is called an ISA. I am worried – is this morally wrong?

John Cole
Acton Trussell, Staffordshire

SIR – As a mere common lawyer I often envied tax practitioners who had persuaded the courts to rise above mundane questions of honesty/dishonesty to consider only avoidance/evasion.

Shoplifters couldn't say: 'I only put the whisky in my pocket to avoid paying, not to evade it.' In the elevated realm of tax, no one asks whether the intention is honest or dishonest.

I sometimes wonder how, if some avoidance scheme were the subject of an indictment, the advice of various tax practitioners – there being no professional privilege in criminal proceedings – would fare in a Crown Court.

Hugh Mayor QC
Hallaton, Leicestershire

SIR – What a fool I've been! For the past fifty years I have been labouring under the misapprehension that the payment of tax was mandatory. Thanks to Starbucks, I now realize that it is voluntary. Put me down for a tenner, Mr Osborne, to cover my liability for the next two years.

Dave I'Anson
Formby, Merseyside

SIR – Rather than boycott Starbucks why not order coffee, sit at a table and stay for as many hours as you like? You are undoubtedly behaving badly but are not doing anything illegal.

Dick Laurence
Wells, Somerset

SIR – Perhaps the country would be better served if the financial directors of Starbucks, Amazon and Google managed its financial affairs.

Bob Cole
Newton Tony, Wiltshire

DID YOU THREATEN TO EAT THE PASTY?

SIR – On Tuesday evening I watched Jeremy Paxman, the *Newsnight* presenter, and two politicians arguing about whether or not David Cameron, the Prime Minister, had purchased a Cornish pasty in Leeds station. It eventually turned out to be Liverpool. Good to know that all is well in the world.

Tony Hill
Stratford-upon-Avon, Warwickshire

SIR — I don't recall anyone asking whether Winston Churchill or Harold Macmillan ate pasties — hot or otherwise.

R. Q.
West Drayton, Middlesex

SIR — We are heating up some pasties. Should we pay VAT? If so, is it on the £1.80 they were originally on sale for, or is it on the 25p my wife paid for them from the reduced-price shelf? Should we send a cheque now or declare it on our tax return?

Charles Leigh-Dugmore
Naphill, Buckinghamshire

SIR — Greggs could allow pasties to cool before selling and provide a microwave for customers to heat their purchases.

Mike Riddles
East Grinstead, West Sussex

SIR — The only time I can recall eating a pasty, I was sitting on a bench overlooking St Ives harbour. Having consumed half of it, I was relieved when a seagull snatched the rest from my hand.

David Miller
Maidenhead, Berkshire

SIR – I remember the good old days when the sign 'hot food' in a pub meant that the cat had been lying on the pies. And jolly tasty they were too.

Alan Castree
Fetcham, Surrey

NEPOTISM IN THE MINES

SIR – Nick Clegg is pandering to fashion in his criticism of nepotism among the elite. Nepotism has always existed at every level of society. Miners, for example, were concerned about the loss of jobs for their sons when pits closed because they had always lobbied for family members to be employed locally. In a small Welsh town some years ago, I was told that only people from three families, or those who attended a certain chapel, could expect to get a job in the local quarry.

I was employed in my school and university holidays by the factory in which my father was a foreman. Many of his workmates had their children working in full-time jobs at the factory.

I suspect Mr Clegg may have a surprise about the extent of nepotism at all levels.

Dr Terry Langford
Milford-on-Sea, Hampshire

SIR — As a result of the government's drive to stamp out nepotism, will my local butcher have to change his sign to 'Joe Bloggs and no son of mine'?

Roger Forrest
Winchester

SIR — I'm so glad that my daughter's career opportunities will not be determined by who my friends are; much better that they be determined by some faceless and unaccountable bureaucrat.

Richard Hughes
Loughton, Buckinghamshire

SIR — David Cameron tells Allison Pearson he is 'very relaxed' about internships. There is an unwelcome tendency for politicians to say they are 'relaxed'. Why can't they 'agree' with something? Does Mr Cameron recline on a chaise longue, surrounded by scented candles and the sound of whale music, when he hears of a friend starting an internship?

This pernicious trend was started by Lord Mandelson, who said New Labour was 'intensely relaxed about people getting filthy rich'. What is the difference between being 'very' and 'intensely' relaxed?

Richard Woodward
Long Eaton, Derbyshire

WORKING HARD VS CHILLAXING

SIR — My wife and I have a dilemma, given that the Conservative Party Conference motto is: 'Hard-working People'. We both balance demanding, full-time jobs with family life, but find that we have carelessly, it seems, worked rather too hard to continue to receive child benefit, or indeed the proposed married couple's tax break. Clearly, we need to learn to slow down, or indeed chillax, a little.

Simon Millar
Poole, Dorset

SIR — I am sure that, come the end of the party-conference season, somebody will have made a tally of how often the word 'hard-working' has been used. This empirical evidence could then be used as a basis for legislation to ban it.

Jeremy C. N. Price
Cromarty

SIR — At what point do hard-working people become non-hard-working people, and lose Mr Cameron's support?

George Noon
Preston, Lancashire

SIR – What about those who don't have families? Do our lords and masters think they sit all day on sofas eating fudge?

Pam Gillham
Sevenoaks, Kent

GRANNY ATTACKS

SIR – Surely the so-called Granny tax is merely a convoluted way of withdrawing the winter fuel allowance?

Barbara Dewick
Bookham, Surrey

SIR – I will happily give up my television licence, bus pass and winter fuel allowance, if the government restores the loss of investment income I am incurring due to their failure to control our banking system.

Peter de Snoo
Truro, Cornwall

SIR – Today is my eightieth birthday, and I understand that that nice Mr Osborne is marking this milestone by giving me an extra 25 pence every week to top up my state pension. Just think: next week I shall be able to afford a stamp, with which to post him a letter of thanks.

Bryan Lillywhite
Mollington, Oxfordshire

SIR – David Cameron wants to help us old people to downsize. I am already two inches shorter than I used to be, so I don't need his help.

John de Lange
London N12

SIR – We are comfortably retired here on the east coast of Yorkshire, both in our seventies and reasonably fit. On reading your front page today my wife quietly but firmly exclaimed, 'We may have downsized, but I'm not going back to f****** work.'

Thomas Robertson
Bridlington, East Yorkshire

SIR – Why not let the elderly run the country instead of the current bunch and solve two problems at one stroke?

Priscilla Thomas
Rode, Somerset

SIR – Nick Clegg wants 'millionaire pensioners' to sacrifice their free bus passes and television licences. Does he believe that 'millionaire pensioners' spend their time jumping on and off buses and watching *Coronation Street*?

Chris Watson
Carlton River, Tasmania, Australia

SIR – When fantasizing about 'wealth' taxes, which dis-incentivize the wealth creators, Nick Clegg might note a quotation from a former one-time Liberal. 'I contend that for a nation to try to tax itself into prosperity is like a man standing in a bucket and trying to lift himself up by the handle,' said Winston Churchill.

Crombie Glennie
Hawksworth, Nottinghamshire

SIR – Why don't we old folk just belt up and try to help? We have had it so good. Many of us could well afford to buy our daily aspirin from the chemist, pay for our own Viagra and send back the winter heating allowance in order to support those in real need.

Come on, guys, we know who we are.

Christopher Richardson
London N7

CAMERON'S DEAR JOHN LETTER

SIR – This is the answer that David Cameron should have proposed for Ed Miliband to give 'John', a City banker concerned that next year's bonus might be capped at £2 million.

'Dear John, You must be a remarkable person to justify your salary and bonus. I am totally delighted that you are earning these sums, as the Treasury is benefiting enormously from your earnings. On your £2 million bonus you will be contributing £1 million in income tax. This is enough to pay for at least twenty-five nurses or teachers. If your employer had not paid you this amount, it would only have paid corporation tax at a much lower rate on its increased profits. Keep up the good work.'

Allan Treacy
Cambridge

SIR – Those who protest at the 'obscene' City bonuses never seem to object to the even more 'obscene' salaries paid to footballers. Why?

Ted Robinson
Harvington, Worcestershire

SIR – As far as I am concerned, Mr Hester may have his bonus and Mr Goodwin his knighthood in exchange for the removal of the RBS Group logo from the centre of the pitches on which Six Nations games are played.

John Carter
Bromley, Kent

SIR – My wife and I, though impoverished, would be quite happy for Mr Hester to keep his bonus, provided that he coughed up £1,000 to buy himself a decent pair of hunting boots. His present cheapos are a sartorial and sporting disgrace.

Roland Fernsby
Furneux Pelham, Hertfordshire

SIR – If the get-rich-quick riff-raff are encouraged to go into banking this is what you must expect. Banking used to be an honourable profession.

Duncan Rayner
Sunningdale, Berkshire

SIR – The rationale for the high salaries of bankers has been that it is necessary to obtain people of the right calibre. I would prefer people of a different calibre.

Mik Shaw
Goring-by-Sea, West Sussex

THE SINISTER SEMANTICS OF FRACKING

SIR – We have at our disposal unlimited cheap energy for at least two generations and all we can do is carp and bicker and doubt. I am convinced that a large part of the problem is the dissonant and sinister name shale gas extraction has been lumbered with: fracking.

A rebranding is called for, with the process given a new, homely, nostalgic name – scrumping, perhaps, or something with an environmental tinge like, well, greening.

Graham Weeks
Vilassar de Mar, Barcelona, Spain

SIR – If, as Anglicans object, fracking puts at risk God's glorious creation, why haven't they previously questioned mining, oil and gas extraction, deep wells, diverted streams and canals and the use of highly polished jewels in Christian ceremonies?

David Thompson
Ipswich, Suffolk

SIR – In 1917 at Manchester University Ernest Rutherford split the atom. Just under 100 years later this country hires a French company to build a nuclear power station with Chinese money.

Eric Slater
Hazel Grove, Cheshire

SIR – The world economy is like a game of Monopoly. The Chinese, Indians and Arabs have got all the money and the best property; we've got the Old Kent Road.

P. J. Minns
Frilford, Oxfordshire

THE WAITROSE INDEX

SIR – David Cameron declares that Aldi's expansion plans are a vote of confidence in the government's economic policies. They could more accurately be seen as a result of this country's recent economic decline, driving shoppers to look for cheaper ways to feed themselves.

True recovery will be apparent when 'hard-working families' begin to return to Waitrose and Sainsbury's, and the food banks close for lack of customers.

Kevin Wright
Harlow, Essex

SIR – Small wonder that many supermarkets are suffering. A family can only consume so much food per week, yet more and more stores keep opening.

Instead of redundant outlets, these sites should have been given over to new housing, relieving the pressure on our precious green countryside.

Margaret Whelband
Barrow upon Soar, Leicestershire

HELP TO SLUMP

SIR – I wonder whether the government has properly assessed the long-term risks associated with its so-called Help to Buy scheme.

The abolition of joint mortgage interest relief at source in 1988 (a scheme designed to make home ownership more affordable in a high-interest-rate environment) led to a spike in house prices as buyers scrambled to pool their allowances before the perk was taken away. The post-abolition slump left many of those buyers in long-term negative equity.

A sustainable recovery in the housing market should be achievable in a low-interest-rate environment without short-termist (and dare one say 'populist') schemes which encourage the assumption of high levels of personal debt and the underwriting of that personal debt by the already overburdened taxpayer.

Iain Thomas
Tunbridge Wells, Kent

SIR – George Osborne's plan for garden cities sounds so delightful, but I can't help thinking that with the economic restrictions and limited land available they will end up more city than garden.

Anne Newbery
Chalfont St Peter, Buckinghamshire

SIR – Last year parents with grown-up children were urged to downsize. Now Mr Cameron wants to remove housing benefit for the under-twenty-fives, effectively telling them that they will have to move back with their parents.

Much as my wife and I love our sons, we do not want them sharing our bedroom.

Richard Tracey
Dinan, Côtes-d'Armor, France

SIR – People born in the sixties and seventies may well find it harder to save money for a flat or house than their parents; they may — but I have my doubts — be worse off than their parents' generation.

However, as a member of the baby boom generation, which seems to get so much flak from those younger than us, I would like to point out that we rarely took family holidays; buying a television was a major investment; few ate out at anything grander than fish and chip shops; clubbing wasn't really invented yet; most households restricted phone calls because of their cost; and credit — including mortgages — was hard to come by, especially if you were a woman. Does the younger generation still think it's hard done by?

Marcia MacLeod

London NW6

3. Those Who Can't,
Legislate

NO ONE FORGETS A GOOD FACILITATOR

SIR – The latest edition of *Around Kent*, a propaganda sheet put out by Kent County Council, refers to the Building Schools for the Future programme in the following terms: 'The days of traditional, stand at the front and give 'em the knowledge teaching are now long gone . . . New teaching spaces which look a bit like plazas are open flexible spaces where students can gather in groups and work together. There are comfy chairs . . . Teachers are facilitators rather than following the more static approach to teaching.'

This is the pernicious rubbish that pervades the education establishment. Michael Gove needs to root it out.

Michael Bright
Tunbridge Wells, Kent

SIR – Why do politicians seem to prefer replacing unsatisfactory school buildings, but not unsatisfactory school teachers? My children and I were taught in grotty – mostly Victorian – classrooms and got a very good education. Many of the present generation leave shining schools with a less than shining fund of knowledge.

Andrew Stobart
Leominster, Herefordshire

SIR — Why is it that in our schools' appraisal system 'satisfactory' is considered unsatisfactory?

Malcolm Macleod-Carey
Newbury, Berkshire

SIR — It was so good to read that pupils will be penalized for bad spelling, grammar and punctuation.

It would be even better news if they were penalized for poor pronunciation.

Clare M. Blake
Sutton, Surrey

SIR — I well remember writing an essay in junior school and asking my teacher how to spell 'yacht'.

There was a pause and then she replied: 'Don't you mean boat?'

C. M. Sturdy
Westward Ho!, Devon

SIR — On more than one occasion my son's not unattractive head teacher has written asking us to bare with her.

Stephen Saunders
Midhurst, West Sussex

SIR – At least Mr Saunders's son has a head teacher. At my children's school, the head is known as 'Head Learner'.

Parents and teachers argue as to who is the learner – the teacher or the pupil. The parents seem pretty clear.

James Gregory
Newton Thornbury, Gloucestershire

SIR – I may start to have faith in our politicians' determination to improve the state school system when they all start using it for their own children.

Until that day I shall just have to follow their example and buy my way round it.

David Armstrong
Hipperholme, West Yorkshire

SIR – Michael Gove, the Education Secretary, is keen to improve the nation's grammar. Last week, I tried to order a ham and cheese panino. After a moment's silence, I was told that they only sold paninis [*sic*]. When I said that this was impossible, I discovered that grammatical accuracy does not win you friends.

Charles Janz
London SW14

SIR – I am very disappointed that Michael Gove has been moved from education, as I believe that he did an excellent job. One way to measure this is by looking at the people he upset: the teaching unions and the Lib Dems.

David Miller
Maidenhead, Berkshire

SIR – Has anyone else noticed that the Department for Education has been staffed largely by Nicks? Nick Gibb on schools, Nick Boles on 'Skills' (whatever that means), and Nicky Morgan as Education Secretary. What is the significance of this?

Daniel Deasy
Oxford

THE MPS' ACADEMY

SIR – It is ironic that Nick Clegg is demanding that teachers in free schools are properly trained and qualified. No Member of Parliament receives any training, and Mr Clegg's only qualification to be Deputy Prime Minister is that he was elected as leader of his party by its own members.

Major David Riddick (retd)
Cranbrook, Kent

SIR – 'Cameron: we need elitism in schools' – like a hole in the head.

Richard W. Symonds
Crawley, West Sussex

SIR – David Cameron's ideas on education require a slogan of corresponding worth. Might I suggest: 'Elitism for all?'

Rory Souter
Coleshill, Warwickshire

THE PRICE OF A 2:2 IN FROLICKING

SIR – It is reported that the combined cost of a three-year degree with living expenses is expected to rise to about £80,000.

Graduates can expect to earn £100,000 more than non-graduates over their lifetimes. Students would, therefore, appear to be trading three years of hard slog – albeit possibly offset against copious amounts of beer and frolicking (which many non-students have anyway) – for a mere £20,000 over more than forty years, or less than £500 per year.

They must be asking themselves if it's worth it.

Bruce Denness
Whitwell, Isle of Wight

SIR – Why not bring up to date the medieval scholastic year of six months in residence and six months of holidays and cut total costs by up to a third? When it took days or even weeks to travel from Oxford or Cambridge, long breaks were necessary, but now, why not follow the lead of the University of Buckingham and offer two-year honours degrees?

Ron Rumble
Hemel Hempstead, Hertfordshire

SIR – Most nurseries and crèches look after toddlers from 9 a.m. till 5 p.m., forty-eight weeks a year. They also provide lunch and tea.

My daughter, currently in her second year at Bristol University, has two hours of lectures a week for thirty-eight weeks a year. I estimate that this works out at approximately £40 per hour.

Her day school cost £175 per week, or £5 per hour. University education doesn't seem such a bargain now, does it?

Elaine McKeith
Cullercoats, Northumberland

SIR – David Cameron trumpeted a £200 tax break for married couples on the very day when thousands of us were dropping off our children at university, to face an £18,000 fees hike over a three-year course.

If he doesn't expect us to feel as if we are being treated as fools, what does he expect?

John Tipping
Chalfont St Peter, Buckinghamshire

SIR – While Nick Clegg found it impossible to stick to his pre-election pledge not to raise tuition fees, I shall find it easy to stick to my post-election one: I vowed never to vote Lib Dem again.

Sian Wyn-Jones
Minchinhampton, Gloucestershire

TEACHING BRITISH VALUES

SIR – David Cameron says that 'British values' should be taught in schools. The BAE scandal of a few years ago centred on suggested bribery payments. The SFO anti-corruption investigation into this was essentially terminated in 2006 by the then prime minister and his government.

What praiseworthy British value was the government displaying by taking that action?

Dr Bob Turvey
Bristol

SIR – 'The chief and governing purpose is to declare our belief and trust in the British way of life, not with any boastful self-confidence nor with any aggressive self-advertisement, but with sober and humble trust that by holding fast to that which is good and rejecting from our midst that which is evil we may continue to be a nation at unity with itself and of service to the world' – official book for the Festival of Britain, 1951.

Patricia Gilpin
Dulverton, Somerset

SIR – According to my television, the dominant British values are simple: 1) food; 2) football; 3) quiz games; 4) antiques.

Gerard Hodkinson
Wetherby, West Yorkshire

SIR – I wonder whom Mr Cameron would least like to implement plans to teach British values in schools – Sepp Blatter or Jean-Claude Juncker?

Philip Moger
East Preston, West Sussex

4. Brussels Doubts

THE EU IS NOT JUST FOR CHRISTMAS

SIR – François Hollande, the President of France, has told David Cameron that Europe, meaning the EU, is 'for life'.

I would sooner have a dog.

Mike Bridgeman
Market Lavington, Wiltshire

SIR – David Cameron said: 'We need to get out of this idea that Britain is committed to ever closer union.' This provision is in Title I, Article A of the Maastricht Treaty, which Britain signed on 7 February 1992.

A. W. Maude
Sutton-in-Craven, West Yorkshire

SIR – May I add to the laurels of your excellent political department by leaking a copy of the Prime Minister's speech on Europe?

It will run as follows: 'Blah, blah, waffle, waffle . . . influence in the corridors of power . . . lunching [*sic*] above our weight . . . stranded in mid Atlantic . . . I know better than the British people, which is why I am determined not to allow them to express their opinion . . . the

political class does very well out of Brussels . . . you proles
can stuff it . . . blah, blah, waffle, waffle.'

Peter Croft
Cambridge

SIR – Regardless of rebellions and rhetoric, every government since 1970 has taken us ever further into Europe.
This one promises to be no different.

Alec Ellis
Liverpool

SIR – 'EU must change or we quit' says your headline on
Oliver Letwin's remarks. I have a better idea: we quit now
and rejoin if it does change.

Brian Gilbert
Hampton, Middlesex

SIR – Persuading twenty-six other countries to 'reform'
the EU is about as likely to succeed as is David Cameron
standing in a herd of wildebeest trying, by an effort of
will, to turn them into gazelles.

Mick Andrews
Doncaster, West Yorkshire

SIR – Charles Moore says, regarding the UK's adherence to the then EEC, that 'people have increasingly come to believe they were lied to'.

They were lied to. I took part in the Commons debates and the referendum of 1975, and, along with others opposed to membership, explained time and again that this was only a step towards a United States of Europe where sovereignty was not 'shared', in the weasel word of that time, but 'transferred'.

Nothing has changed. People continue to be duped or lied to over a renegotiation that is likely, as in 1975, to be designed to leave the Brussels project untouched.

Jim Sillars (MP 1970–79 and 1988–92)
Edinburgh

SIR – Laurent Fabius, the French Foreign Minister, likens Britain's stance on the EU to joining a football club and then telling the other members you want to play rugby.

What happens if you join a football club wanting to play football, but the others decide that they want to play rugby?

John Shields
London SW1

SIR – The EU operates in the same way as FIFA. Everyone knows both organizations are mismanaged by second-rate people, but the members don't want to rock the boat in case they miss out on the perks.

Laurence Heath
Wokingham, Berkshire

SIR – François Hollande thinks we should stick to the *prix fixe* menu rather than pick and choose from the *à la carte* menu. That would be all right if the restaurateur didn't keep sticking on extras and upping the price. The menu I voted for in 1975 bears little resemblance to that from which we are now being force-fed.

Ron Giddens
Caterham, Surrey

SIR – The EU might make better decisions if it held meetings during the day, after a good English breakfast, rather than all night after a gross French dinner.

Michael Noar
Hollingbourne, Kent

SIR – You report a French diplomat as saying that Britain was 'like a man who wants to go to a wife-swapping party without taking his own wife'.

Surely we would rather not associate too closely with disgusting people like these.

Tom Foster
Kelvedon, Essex

WEEKEND MEMBERSHIP

SIR — At my golf club there are different categories of membership, including a discounted country member-ship for those who live at some distance from the club.

I am sure the United Kingdom is far enough away from Brussels to qualify.

Harry Stevens
Upper Bentley, Worcestershire

SIR — Your correspondent believes that the country should be given the choice of being ruled by Westminster or Brussels. In other words, democracy or bureaucracy.

John Strange
Worthing, West Sussex

SIR — The EU is beginning to resemble Austria-Hungary: imperious, undemocratic, unpopular and bankrupt.

We should not be fettered to a corpse.

David Lane
Kidderminster, Worcestershire

SIR — It is obviously expedient for Eurosceptics to promote their view that, by leaving the EU, the British will 'get their country back'. But British foreign policy has not been independent since the end of the Second World War; it has been led by America. When Britain has tried to pursue an independent policy that went against the interests of the United States — Suez for example — it has proven disastrous.

Britain's trade policy will continue to be led by decisions made in Brussels, given how important the EU market will continue to be for British businesses, and given how slow British businesses have been to exploit opportunities in China and India, for example (unlike the Germans and the French).

De Gaulle was right; Britain should never have joined the EU; getting out now would, however, be an even greater mistake.

Bharat Jashanmal
Fairford, Gloucestershire

SIR — Mary Riddell uses the metaphor of Britain being eaten alive by a bear if it exits from the EU.

A more apt image is that of Jonah and the whale. We have already been swallowed by the EU and now seek regurgitation.

Peter Haworth
Clitheroe, Lancashire

SIR – Professor Michael Oakeshott's essay 'Rationalism in Politics' contains a wonderful sentence: 'The politicians of Europe pore over the simmering banquet they are preparing for the future; but, like jumped-up kitchen porters deputizing for an absent cook, their knowledge does not extend beyond the written word which they read mechanically — it generates ideas in their heads but no taste in their mouths.'

Oakeshott warned us that those who seek to plan society from a textbook and from the top will always fail. We now witness the politicians of Europe starved of ideas to sort out a mess they have created.

James Adam Paton
Billericay, Essex

SIR – The essential question about the European Union is whether we would let our children die for it. My grandfather fought in the Great War, my father in the Second World War, and my son did three tours of Iraq, all for values embodied in Queen and country. The idea that our children would fight and die at the behest of Herman Van Rompuy, and all the values he embodies, is absurd.

Brian Milton
London E2

JUNCKER'S HEROICS

SIR – It's a little disappointing if the worst the sceptics can find to say about Jean-Claude Juncker, the potential President of the European Commission, is that he has cognac for breakfast. If true, it is a foible which would have endeared him to Dr Johnson, who wrote: 'Claret is the liquor for boys, port for men, but he who aspires to be a hero must drink brandy.'

Charles Keen

Duntisbourne Rouse, Gloucestershire

SIR – The good news about the appointment of Juncker is that he seems well qualified to organize a booze-up in a brewery – one task, among many, that has eluded the Commission since its inception.

Richard Endacott

Reading, Berkshire

SIR – We are often told by Europhiles that the reason Britain must stay in the European Union is that, if we left, we would have no influence; the naming of Jean-Claude Juncker as President of the European Commission shows we have none anyway. We might just as well leave at the earliest opportunity and pocket the £50 million-plus-per-day it costs us to be ignored.

Ian Goddard

Wickham, Hampshire

SIR – The game used to be to ask the names of three famous Belgians. Should we now be asking the same question in relation to Luxembourgeois?

Richard Hardman
Standford, Hampshire

SIR – Walking up the High Street in Newport, Shropshire, one Saturday morning in 1941 with friends from a nearby school, we saw a lorry loaded with the remains of a German Junkers 88 bomber. We could not resist helping ourselves to a small souvenir.

Should I offer the broken fragment of a Junkers' fuselage to the Prime Minister to brighten the Cabinet Room table?

Sydney Preston
Sevenoaks, Kent

SIR – Although I hate to admit it, I have to side with EU chief Jean-Claude Juncker when he says David Cameron has no common sense. Cameron may have had an Eton education, but he has zilch up top. No way would I trust him on the battlefield. He would be a disaster.

Lt Col Dale Hemming-Tayler (retd)
Edith Weston, Rutland

YES! YES! YES!

SIR — The head of the Civil Service is looking for ideas to make Britain happy. A simple 'in' or 'out' referendum on our membership of the EU would make at least half of Britain not just happy but utterly ecstatic.

Mike Bridgeman
Devizes, Wiltshire

SIR — Those of us who took David Cameron at face value in 2007, when he issued his 'cast iron guarantee' over a referendum on the Lisbon Treaty, are unlikely to be impressed with his suggestion that 'fresh consent' should be sought from the electorate once Britain's relationship with Europe has 'crystallized', whatever that means.

Mr Cameron reminds me of A. A. Milne's ship-wrecked old sailor, who 'did nothing but bask until he was saved'.

Alasdair Ogilvy
Iping, West Sussex

SIR — We are told by Mr Cameron that he is going to do this, that and another. Would it be impertinent to ask: when?

John A. Jones
Swansea

SIR – Edward Heath must be satisfied on his cloud, listening to a loop of 'Ode to Joy' and reflecting on his betrayal of Britain. It is now clear that no British government will ever allow a referendum on membership of the EU – never, ever, ever.

Tony Greatorex
Syston, Leicestershire

SIR – Many seem to have forgotten that Harold Wilson won an election by offering renegotiation with Europe followed by a referendum. There was precious little of the former and when it came to the latter, all the main political parties together with the full force of the government machine were mobilized to ensure the outcome.

If David Cameron wins again, we are surely in for a repeat performance.

The only way out of the EU is to elect a majority of Eurosceptic MPs to Westminster.

Richard Moorfield
Threshfield, North Yorkshire

SIR – Why not have a referendum to decide whether we have a referendum on Europe?

G. R. Skeates
Budleigh Salterton, Devon

SIR — I believe that I have a suggestion for an in/out European referendum that will satisfy all parties and could be carried out well before the next election. I refer to the Eurovision Song Contest.

Surely even Nick Clegg could be expected to join the rest of Britain in voting to preserve our sanity and dignity by extricating ourselves from this humiliation.

John Ellis
Truro, Cornwall

SIR — Your letters on the EU are really arguing for a revolution right now: dumping the coalition government, parking David Cameron in the Tower, and taking back power by the people.

I would be pleased to lead this movement if nobody else better qualified can be found — which should not be hard, since I am on the cusp of my eighty-eighth year and spend most of my time in my garden.

Lord Walsingham
Merton, Norfolk

SIR — The authors of several letters on this page have urged, and continue to urge, that David Cameron call a national referendum without further delay. But a referendum requires an Act of Parliament to set it up.

Nick Clegg would certainly use his blocking vote in the Commons to prevent that. The phalanx of Lib Dem and Labour peers in the Lords, some of them on the Brussels payroll and disgracefully refusing to acknowledge a conflict of interest, would seek to do the same there.

That is why Mr Cameron must await the outcome of the next general election and hope he returns with a working majority.

There is no point in baying for the moon.

Frederick Forsyth
Beaconsfield, Buckinghamshire

SIR – Browsing the letters page today I notice that all the letters about *Les Misérables* are written by women and all the letters written about the EU referendum are from men. Was this deliberate?

Ruth Cliff
Uckfield, East Sussex

EU'S BUDGET BAILIFFS

SIR – The President of the European Commission, Jean-Claude Juncker, has threatened us with a fine if we refuse to pay £1.75 billion. If we refuse to pay the fine, too, what will he do – send in the bailiffs?

Robert Readman
Bournemouth, Dorset

SIR – If I were David Cameron or George Osborne, I would tell the European Union that Britain will only pay the extra £850 million now demanded by the EU when last year's accounts are fully signed off by independent auditors who have approved the way the money was spent.

Adam Secretan
Barcombe, East Sussex

SIR – If a man couldn't decide which of two cities, 300 miles apart, to live in, and his solution was to live for a month in each and go to and fro twelve times a year at great expense, he would rightly be regarded as mad.

Yet this is what is costing the EU £93 million a year.

David Cook
Cottingham, East Yorkshire

SIR – The European Commission pronounces that Britain 'continues to experience macroeconomic imbalances which require monitoring and policy action'.

Have its members no sense of irony?

Robert Langford
Coventry, Warwickshire

SIR – I wonder if HMRC will be understanding if I choose to follow the Prime Minister's example and refuse to pay my next VAT bill.

Though I won't include calculations for prostitution or drug dealing in my return.

Michael Powell
Tealby, Lincolnshire

SIR – Politicians of various stripes have been jumping up and down, declaring how unfair it is that, just because the economy has done so well, Britain should pay more money to the EU.

These, surely, can't be the same politicians who think that people who have worked harder should pay more tax?

Geoff Newton
Tighnabruaich, Argyll

SIR – Could you stop describing the Tory MPs who voted against increases in the EU budget as 'rebels'? They were representing the views of their constituents, which every MP is elected to do. They deserve to be commended.

W. G. Blake
Malmesbury, Wiltshire

SIR — You have recently reported on the return of *Star Wars*, Michael Heseltine and now Tory EU rebels.

I'm feeling positively rejuvenated.

Christopher Cox
Taynuilt, Argyllshire

NOT WAVING, BUT DROWNING

SIR — The euro crisis reminds one of the Sergeant's words in *Macbeth*, describing the two opposing sides in the battle from which he has just returned to King Duncan as 'two spent swimmers that do cling together / And choke their art'.

The debt-ridden nations of the EU, like drowning men, are too exhausted to go it on their own and will continue to pull down all others in their downward spiral.

Michael R. Gordon
Bewdley, Worcestershire

SIR — I just don't get it. The euro is in dire straits but I still have to pay 90 pence to buy one. Why?

Robert Warner
West Woodhay, Berkshire

SIR — A 100-peseta coin in the church collection on Sunday. Is this a sign?

Julian Burtt
Henley-on-Thames, Oxfordshire

SIR — Just back from 'impoverished' northern Spain. Fantastic new roads, new towns replacing fishing villages, and no parking spaces for the huge increase in vehicles. No evidence of their so-called economic problems.

B. F. Hunt
Broadstone, Dorset

SIR — I see in your Cyprus Bailout Live blog, at 13:55, a reference to the 'Finish [*sic*] Europe Minister'. Thank goodness it is all over.

Brian Gilbert
Hampton, Middlesex

SIR — Thinking that I needed some basic background reading to understand better the eurozone crisis, I visited the Amazon website to look for a suitable volume.

I found a book by searching under the title *The European Union for Dummies*, but it only seems to be available in German.

Stephen Jones
London SE19

SIR — Change in the eurozone is now inevitable. A realignment of the currency into a Greek Orthodox euro, a Catholic euro and a Protestant euro would accord with historic choices and current economic reality. Britain might even opt in.

Dr John Doherty
Vienna, Austria

SIR — Gordon Brown got us in a right financial mess, but I forgive him all that for keeping us out of the euro.

John Lewis
Cheltenham, Gloucestershire

SIR — MEPs have taken no part in the deliberations on the euro crisis, and are unlikely to contribute to any solution. What is the point of the European Parliament?

Tony Ellis
Northwood, Middlesex

SIR — At present is it not a little dishonest that Euro-leaders should look so happy and smiling in their group photographs?

David Knapman
Taunton, Somerset

SIR — Surely all the ministers and delegates staying up until 4 a.m. broke EU working-time directives, and therefore any decisions are invalid.

Helen Wynne-Griffith
London W8

SIR — European politicians remind me of Auberon Waugh's words: 'Until the public accepts that the urge to power is a personality disorder in its own right, like the taste for rubber underwear, there will always be the danger of circumstances arising which persuade people to start listening to politicians and taking them seriously.'

James Preston
Madrid

HOW TO MAKE A GREEK SALAD

SIR — One is, of course, delighted to hear that the Greek economy is to be saved — once again. On a recent visit to Crete I asked for the recipe for a Greek salad. There came the not entirely ironic reply: 'First, you borrow some feta . . .'

Christopher Rodda
Boscastle, Cornwall

SIR — It seems appropriate that the words 'crisis' and 'chaos' are of Greek origin.

Geoff Eley
Dunmow, Essex

SIR — The Greek referendum on the EU debt deal is scheduled for some time in January 2012. Do we yet know the date for the second referendum which will no doubt be required when the Greeks get the answer wrong at the first attempt?

Earl of Ronaldshay
Aske, North Yorkshire

SIR — Greece could be helped if Germany returned the gold it stole in the last war, worth $97 billion at today's prices.

Elizabeth Parker
Longtown, Cumbria

DETERMINED DAVE

SIR – David Cameron is determined. Determined to win back the Rochester and Strood constituency; determined to claw back sovereign powers from Brussels; determined to deal with immigration.

It's a pity that he cannot convert that determination into concrete results.

Sandy Pratt
Dormansland, Surrey

SIR – Every week, it seems, we hear what 'David Cameron thinks' or 'David Cameron says'. When are we going to read that David Cameron has actually done something?

Don Minterne
Bradford Peverell, Dorset

SIR – I see absolutely no reason to believe that David Cameron and his party of jelly-spined jobsworths are qualified or able to negotiate with the EU.

Christopher L. Cruden
Lugano, Ticino, Switzerland

SIR – Your correspondent may well be right about the intelligence and charm of Bulgarian would-be immigrants, but she doesn't explain where we are supposed to put them all.

I live in one of the numerous areas in the country threatened with large-scale development because of the increasing need for houses.

Our countryside is vanishing, we are running out of space to bury our dead and our rubbish, we are currently the second most overcrowded country in Europe and all Vince Cable can do is produce the 'racist' card. It's not race, Mr Cable, it's numbers.

Maggie Hughes
Gnosall, Staffordshire

SIR – The emigration of Vince Cable would make a welcome addition to the net immigration target proposed by Mr Cameron.

John Wheatley
Hanbury, Worcestershire

SIR – 'Cable compares Cameron to Enoch Powell'. If only . . .

John Carlisle (Conservative MP 1979–97)
Sevenoaks, Kent

SIR – Michael Howard made immigration one of the key planks of the Conservatives' 2005 general election campaign. They lost.

Hugh Payne
Hitchin, Hertfordshire

SIR – Perhaps those who advocate ever stricter immigration controls should remember that, for two years, Jesus and his family were, effectively, immigrants and asylum seekers in Egypt?

Dr Nick Winstone-Cooper
Laleston, Mid Glamorgan

SIR – My experience of immigrants in the workplace is that they are dedicated, hard-working and responsible. If David Cameron spent more time addressing the problem of our own workshy nationals we might all be better off.

Richard Jones
Bury St Edmunds, Suffolk

SIR – I note that EU migrants may soon have to sign in at police stations. If any of them manage to find a police station still open, perhaps they would let me know.

Philip Moger
Preston, West Sussex

5. All Noisy on the Home Front

THE STUDENTS ARE REVOLTING . . .

SIR – I can't get excited about these students protesting. Compared to the first and second Grosvenor Square demonstrations in 1968, this lot are pussy cats. Most of the students who travelled to London with me in 1968 got arrested, injured or laid, and in some cases, all three.

Philip Saunders
Ditchingham Dam, Suffolk

SIR – May I suggest that if the police are to use water cannons to disperse rioting students, they include some soap in the tank?

Finlay Mason
Luxembourg

SIR – Never mind scrapping Boris Johnson's water cannons: I'd ask the mayoral candidates if I could play with one.

Nigel Griffiths
London NW4

. . . AND SO IS EVERYONE ELSE

SIR – Having taught our children that there is no absolute right and wrong; having assured them that relationships, like Lego, can be formed and broken at a whim; having told them that he who has the most wins; having severed a generation from all that is true and right and good and lovely – why should the riots come as any surprise? We have reaped what we have sown.

Revd Gerard Hemmings
Twickenham, Middlesex

SIR – Is this what a godless society looks like?

Judith Davies
Worcester

SIR – Why are the parents of these children not also in the dock? If it were their dogs behaving in this fashion, they would be liable to prosecution.

R. Duncan Ferguson
Castle Douglas, Galloway

SIR – The 'What I did in the summer holidays' essays should make for interesting reading this year.

Paul McCaffrey
London NW5

SIR – When David Cameron delivered his Big Society speech on 19 July 2010, he must have had in mind something completely different from the events of the past week: 'The Big Society is about a huge culture change where people, in their everyday lives, in their homes, in their neighbourhoods, in their workplace, don't always turn to officials, local authorities or central government for answers to the problems they face, but instead feel both free and powerful enough to help themselves . . .'

Bruce Chalmers
Goring-by-Sea, West Sussex

SIR – How comforting that, once again, it's only a small minority.

Martin Burgess
Beckenham, Kent

SIR – Oh no! I have a hoodie on, where's the nearest Currys? I am eighteen and I find suggestions that all hoodie owners are vandals highly insulting. Even my dad has a hoodie, and as far as I know, he hasn't come home with a new TV and microwave.

Richard Sharples
Blackburn, Lancashire

SIR – In 1780 a brutal mob took over London for nearly a fortnight. Arson, robbery and violence prevailed, virtually unchecked.

Samuel Johnson witnessed some of the robbers at work: 'They were not I believe a hundred; but they did their work at leisure, in full security, without sentinels, without trepidation, as men lawfully employed in full day.'

As today, the authorities proved too incompetent or timid to repress the riots. Almost alone among those in authority to retain his courage and presence of mind was King George III, who eventually took it upon himself to order in the Guards. Thereupon, the violence was suppressed in short time.

Sadly, today we have no George III, and nothing suggests that such hellish scenes will not be repeated. The criminal classes have learnt that they are all but free to prey upon the population at large.

Nikolai Tolstoy
Southmoor, Berkshire

SIR – Appearing on *Question Time*, Dr John Sentamu, the Archbishop of York, was unequivocal in his support of the right of an individual to defend his family and property from would-be looters.

During the Gordon Riots of 1780, Archbishop William Markham fought his way into the House of Lords with his fists, and on his return home set about arming his servants with weapons in order to repel any rioters with designs on his house.

I wonder if Dr Sentamu has taken inspiration from his sturdy predecessor.

Serenhedd James
Oxford

SIR – David Cameron proposes that gang leaders should be given hell, by being pursued relentlessly for payment of television licences, parking fines, council tax and so on. That should certainly make them feel they're part of society, since this is exactly how the rest of us are treated.

William Wilson
London SE5

SIR – In spite of the riots in our towns and cities I didn't see any looters nicking a duck house.

Valda Mossman
Newlyn, Cornwall

SIR – As a magistrate of thirty years' service I often wish I had had the sentencing powers in a science fiction book I once read, in which the miscreant was beamed into the Middle Ages to undergo the stocks.

Adrian Holloway
Minchinhampton, Gloucestershire

SIR – The Big Stick Society?

Lt Col Martin Burton (retd)
Little Barningham, Norfolk

SIR – None of the discussion about the recent widespread riots has mentioned that rioting and smashing things up is fun. When the blood's up and you're running in the herd, the darker side of animal instincts is ready to take over.

The challenge, therefore, is to create a suitable policy to outweigh this. Three years' military service on conviction for rioting should do it.

If the idea of the Army is too much for you (or for the Army), then three applications of the Taser at monthly intervals might also have a modestly effective outcome.

We don't need to bring back the birch.

J. C.
Great Malvern, Worcestershire

SIR — The average private in the Army is paid £24,381 to risk death in Afghanistan, protecting a corrupt government.

Metropolitan Police figures show that the average police officer is paid £31,176, to stand and watch criminals burn and loot.

Frank Thomas
Bristol

SIR — With regards to the numerous calls for the Army to be used in times of riot, it may be worth noting that the purpose of our police is to protect the community and serve the people, while that of the Armed Forces is to engage the enemies of the state. History shows that when the Armed Forces become the police, then the people often become the enemies of the state.

Joseph Arnold Davey
Whickham, Northumberland

SIR – If we cannot regain control of our cities, we will have to appoint Tony Blair as a peace envoy to ourselves.

Hillary Bagshaw
Portsmouth, Hampshire

SIR – I learnt yesterday that 'the South African government is advising people to postpone trips to Britain because of the violence'. The pendulum has swung.

Christine Suddick
Stratford-upon-Avon, Warwickshire

SIR – It is said that during the Indian Mutiny, the rebels communicated by leaving chapattis on doorsteps. The Raj was too sensible to try to ban chapattis. Now, in the post-chapatti era, Mr Cameron should be equally wary of closing down social media such as Twitter and Facebook.

Tim Hedges
Rome

SIR – Here in Crickhowell we had our own version of the recent riots. A local resident commented to me, grumpily, that the emptying of garden waste bins could often be late. I agreed with him, equally grumpily.

Strangely, it wasn't covered by the media.

Phil Bailey (social delinquent)
Crickhowell, Powys

SIR – While most newspapers this week were writing about the riots, the headline in the *Wiltshire Times* read: 'One-legged belly dancer stages comeback.'

Marion Dewar
Trowbridge, Wiltshire

SIR – People will say I am out of touch, but surely all this rioting and looting will stop when the perpetrators head for the moors tomorrow for the start of the grouse shooting season?

Nicky Samengo-Turner
Hundon, Suffolk

PC PLEB

SIR – I do not understand why there is an outcry over Andrew Mitchell's use of the word 'pleb'. 'Pleb' is a historical term for a commoner, in the same way that

'gentleman' is a historical term for a landowner or armiger
— someone entitled to a coat of arms.

If the policeman is not, as Mr Mitchell suggests, a
plebeian, he has to be either of gentle birth, armigerous
or a landowner. If he can fulfil any of these requirements,
he can safely call himself a gentleman and rightfully take
offence at anyone who calls him a 'pleb', but if he does not
fulfil these requirements, he should not complain.

Edward Kendall
Cranbrook, Kent

SIR — The government minister cannot have used the
word 'pleb'. A patrician would know that the singular
form is 'plebs'.

Richard Ashcroft
Ware, Hertfordshire

SIR — If there is no independent confirmation of the
words spoken then the matter is not worth pursuing. I
once called a neighbour 'unpleasant', and forever more
she said I'd called her 'a peasant'.

Ian Walker
Addingham, West Yorkshire

SIR — If the former Government Chief Whip had used the
classical Greek term *hoi polloi* instead of *pleb* he might have
kept his job. Most dogberries would have assumed he was

talking about a high-street fashion store — but only if he had put the stress on the wrong syllable.

David McA. McKirdy
Mansfield Woodhouse, Nottinghamshire

SIR — As a life-long Classics master now well stricken in years, what amazes me most about the never-ending Plebgate row is the contrast between my own gently disintegrating frame and the astonishing vigour of the Latin language, which retains undimmed the power to shock and outrage with a single word. *Cruda viridisque senectus* indeed!

John Holland
Bedford

SIR — I, as a pleb and a member of the Conservative Party, welcome the Chief Whip's resignation.

George Acheson
Fakenham, Norfolk

SIR — I am sorry Andrew Mitchell has had to resign. By riding a bicycle he was setting a good example by being 'green'. If he had been in a car this matter would not have arisen, as the police would have had to open the main gates for him.

Angela Bayliss
Amesbury, Wiltshire

SIR – I have hitherto regarded myself as a tolerant man, but in the light of recent accusations against Andrew Mitchell, the Chief Whip, and Lance Armstrong, the Tour de France champion, I have now refused to let my daughter marry a cyclist.

Viv Payne
Edwalton, Nottinghamshire

SIR – Andrew Mitchell lost his temper. It happens. He has apologized. In Italy this would be regarded as normal behaviour.

Henrietta Lindsell
Aylsham, Norfolk

SIR – Has Mr Mitchell paid too high a price? Not if we recall that Mr Toad got a year for car theft, three for furious driving, and fifteen for 'cheeking the police', 'which was a bad sort of cheek . . . even if you only believe one-tenth . . . of what you heard'.

Robert Stephenson
Henley-on-Thames, Oxfordshire

SIR – Last night's BBC News showed policemen wearing T-shirts bearing the message 'PC Pleb and proud'. If so, what are they upset about?

Andrew Allen
Mobberley, Cheshire

SIR — I'm amazed how many senior police officers are sociology graduates. Are they in the right job?

Colin Laverick
London WC2

SIR — Is Plebgate the first political scandal to involve an actual gate?

Annie Pierce
Birkenhead, Cheshire

OCCUPYING THE MORAL HIGH GROUND

SIR — The intransigence of the St Paul's protesters damages both the cathedral and the protesters' cause. They have sought an illogical battle with an institution they have no argument with, on a site inappropriate to their concerns.

It would be a fine gesture for the protesters, rather than to show their social concerns by dancing all night, staging a half-term holiday camp and returning to their alternative accommodation when it gets chilly, to go among the poor of our capital and use their energies in providing food, shelter and long-term support: to effect change by proper direct action.

Andrew Green
South Croydon, Surrey

SIR – Your correspondents who criticize the Occupy London protesters for being unclear about the way ahead miss the point. Those participating in the Peasants' Revolt or slave rebellions might not have been able to articulate fully worked-out replacement systems.

The first step has to be to highlight the injustices of the status quo and to encourage politicians and thinkers urgently to seek a better way.

Without the admission of the need for change we will get nowhere.

Andrew Papworth
Billericay, Essex

DRUNK TANKED UP

SIR – David Cameron's suggestion that drunk tanks might help tackle the drinking epidemic looks certain, if enacted, to fall victim to the law of unforeseen consequences.

If young people are anything like they were in my youth, they'll find a night in the drunk tank rather an adventure – particularly if there are no subsequent charges or black marks on their record.

Damien McCrystal
London W14

SIR – It is abundantly clear to anyone visiting Britain that there is a drinking problem which cannot simply be attributed to the abolition of drinking hours.

I see this at my son's university in Scotland. As an

expat, I was shocked to see the change in 'social' drinking habits.

Alcohol, especially spirits, is so much cheaper than thirty-five years ago that students think nothing of ordering several chasers with their pints, which was the exception, not the rule, in my day. For those who worry about their budget, a pre-sortie home binge can be had for a couple of pounds.

Students have always drunk a lot, but now the quantities consumed are truly eye-popping. Restoring real prices to the levels of the 1970s would surely help limit the speed and ferocity of drinking.

Simon Noble
Larchmont, New York, United States

SIR – I am fond of barley wine, which has an alcoholic strength comparable to such lagers as Tennent's Super. I tend to drink it at home, and have never missed a day's work on account of it. Why then should I pay Yob Tax on it?

Stephen Grieve
Reigate, Surrey

SIR – If tax from motorists via fuel and vehicle duty is to be spent on roads, I'd like to see taxes from alcohol used to build more pubs.

Mark Redhead
Oxford

SIR – What's up with these prime ministers? Gordon Brown took away our 100-watt light bulbs and now David Cameron wants to control our drinking.

Geoffrey Bremner
Cookham, Berkshire

SIR – If I drink double the recommended amount of alcohol, it is because I am experiencing only half the quality of life I aspire to.

Chris Wood
York

SIR – I am nearing my eightieth birthday, and no one will tell me what I should or should not drink. My wife and I have a glass or two of wine every night with our evening meal. The idea is not to arrive at the Pearly Gates looking a million dollars, but to be waving a glass of Merlot in one hand and a bar of chocolate in the other saying, 'Whoopee, what a ride.'

Tony Woodcock
Stoke-on-Trent, Staffordshire

REDEFINING MARRIAGE JOKES

SIR – You do realize that the gay marriage bill ruins the only joke I can ever remember: Should a married couple be frank and earnest, or should one be a woman?

Jerry Dixon
Hythe, Kent

SIR – I read that the Bishop of Buckingham has spoken out on the Church's ban on blessings for homosexual partnerships. There must be a limerick somewhere in there.

Hugh Smorfitt
Tichborne, Hampshire

SIR – Will female bishops preside over gay marriage ceremonies?

P. J. Minns
Frilford, Oxfordshire

SIR – David Cameron is determined to push the issue of gay marriage because his wife wants him to.

Nick Clegg may send his son to a private school to avoid upsetting his wife.

Remind me, please, which lady we elected to represent us.

Carmichael A. Thomas
Wellingborough, Northamptonshire

SIR – I can't quite work it out: is Mr Cameron a closet gay or a closet liberal?

P. F.
Wortham, Suffolk

SIR – It seems that not only does David Cameron want to redefine the meaning of marriage but also the meaning of Conservative.

W. P. Kitcat
Abinger, Surrey

SIR – I would hate to be the gay child of any of the many hard-hearted Conservative dignitaries who signed the letter last week against gay marriage.

Michael Plumbe
Hastings, East Sussex

SIR – Since the advent of gay marriage, at our factory we no longer employ men of child-bearing age.

A. C. Ball
Greenfield, Manchester

SIR – Whatever happened to those clever, artistic, interesting queers of my youth? Now they all want to be boring, middle-class, married couples. What is this world coming to?

David Wiltshire
Bedford

SIR – Gays should be able to marry so they can suffer like the rest of us.

Leslie Watson
Swansea

SIR – At one time homosexuality was a capital offence, then deportation and imprisonment became the sanctions. Over the years it was severely frowned upon, followed by merely not being talked about.

It then became accepted and gradually approved of. It seems that today it is almost fashionable. I'm seventy-four and hope to be dead before it becomes compulsory.

Donald Lewis
Gifford, East Lothian

SIR – I cannot believe that people are still arguing against same-sex marriages and against gay couples having the same rights as heterosexual couples.

It wasn't long ago that sex before marriage was considered abhorrent, let alone having a child outside wedlock. Now it is a matter of course that couples live together before getting married and indeed have children without ever getting married or being in a lasting relationship.

In ten years' time, the position will be the same with regard to gay couples and people will wonder what all the fuss was about.

Samantha Hookway
Eastbourne, East Sussex

SIR – Being a devoted husband, as well as a staunch and active member of the Conservative Party, I'd be grateful to learn what further changes it will adopt, especially in regard to monogamy. My wife could do with a bit more help around the house.

Robert Vincent
Wildhern, Hampshire

SUBSTANTIAL FEARMONGERING

SIR – I am sitting at home wondering exactly what it means when Mr Cameron says that the terrorist threat is raised from substantial to severe. Are we all supposed to look behind us a little more when we walk the streets? Do we look in waste bins for explosive objects?

Mick Ferrie
Mawnan Smith, Cornwall

SIR – David Cameron does himself no favours in justifying the government's increasing invasions of our privacy by trotting out the well-worn phrase that it is done to protect us from terrorism. I am surprised that he didn't tell Angela Merkel that 'if she had done nothing wrong, then she had nothing to fear'.

Gerald Payman
Auckland, New Zealand

SIR – Tony Blair's Human Rights Act was passed in 1998. Has speech become freer since then? Is family life more secure? Is the state less intrusive? As another prime minister once said: 'No! No! No!'

Joseph B. Fox
Redhill, Surrey

SIR – At his coronation, King Ethelred II promised that he would 'prohibit all manner of rapine and injustice to men of every condition'. This commitment to human rights dates from the year 978.

Yet now the Home Secretary wishes to set this country against our ancient tradition of respect for the individual by withdrawing from the European Convention on Human Rights. That document has done more good for this country than any short-sighted anxiety over adverse court rulings could ever overcome.

Jeremy Goldsmith
Newark-on-Trent, Nottinghamshire

SIR – When Mrs Thatcher tried to deny terrorists (at that time, the IRA) the 'oxygen of publicity', the BBC broadcast their statements read by actors.

Will the BBC now broadcast the sermons of radical Islamist preachers read out by actors?

W. G. Sellwood
Stafford

SIR – Do you think it will be humanly possible for the BBC to get Abu Qatada on *Thought for the Day* before he buggers off back to Jordan?

Robert Stevenson
Cheltenham, Gloucestershire

RADICAL MORRIS DANCERS

SIR – Imam Dr Taj Hargey writes eloquently and persuasively as to why it is not necessary for Muslims to wear the niqab or the burka, but he misses the fundamental point.

Britain has a proud tradition of persuading, not telling people to do things. It is why the shrinking numbers of Morris dancers have not been forced underground and members have not been radicalized into disrupting village fetes with spoiling tactics.

Banning anything is deeply offensive to the British psyche. In the past fifty years we have had to put up with Teddy boys, rockers, skinheads, punks and Russell Brand.

I am sure we can cope with some people who choose to wear the veil.

Dick Corbett
Winchester, Hampshire

SIR – I wonder how many people are aware that the late President of Syria, Hafez al-Assad, banned the wearing of the veil in the souk in Damascus when he was in power.

Peter Shepheard
Poole, Dorset

6. Corners of Foreign Fields

THE EUROPEAN SPRING

SIR — The last twelve months have proved disastrous for unelected, out of touch and unpopular heads of governments the world over. Hosni Mubarak of Egypt, Gordon Brown of the United Kingdom and Ben Ali of Tunisia have all been toppled.

Let us hope that Robert Mugabe, Mahmoud Ahmadinejad and Baroness Ashton are watching closely and sleeping less easily in their beds tonight.

Vere Bruce-Gardyne
London SW6

SIR — I see David Cameron's Big Society is proving most effective in the Middle East. Does this mean that he will now become an Internationalist like Tony Blair?

Robert C. Osborn
Bideford, Devon

SIR — Your analysis of the Arab Spring is too pessimistic. I have been to Cairo three times since Mubarak fell, in order to encourage the secular liberal party.

While it is true that progress towards democracy is unsteady, it is worlds away from the despotism the Egyptians and other Arabs have suffered for generations, while we turned a blind eye.

My distant relation T. E. Lawrence, who incited the

first Arab revolt, which failed because of British and French duplicity, would have rejoiced at the freedom that Arabs are courageously taking for themselves. At least we and the French are rightly making belated amends in Libya.

Edward McMillan-Scott MEP (Lib Dem)
Brussels

SIR – T. E. Lawrence, upon his return to England, advised the British to leave the Arabs to their own dark and bloody future. Wise words then, as they remain today.

J. A. Whitmore
York

BRITAIN'S MORAL COMPASS POINTS TO LIBYA

SIR – Clement Attlee showed great courage in honouring Britain's 'distant obligation' to protect the people of South Korea from invasion. Now, sixty-one years later, as a result of legal intervention, the Republic of Korea has become a world-class economic and industrial power.

Today Britain has another courageous prime minister, and we have joined other responsible nations, again under the Charter of the United Nations, to ensure that the people of Libya may in the future have freedom to control their own affairs.

Our Armed Forces have already responded to the initial challenge, Parliament has given massive support for action, and our nation can be proud that we have found our 'moral compass' once again.

Lt Col. R. L. T. Jones
Odiham, Hampshire

SIR – William Hague, the Foreign Secretary, is signalling a more muscular foreign policy. Doesn't that require an aircraft carrier or two?

Roger Ellis
Shrewsbury

SIR – I presume that the British contribution to the action will consist of Messrs Cameron, Clegg and Fox standing off the coast of Libya in a pedalo throwing paper darts.

Neil Brook
Cambridge

SIR – The British Prime Minister and the French President wrote to the EU President to suggest Gaddafi 'should leave'. The Foreign Secretary wrote to the UN Secretary to suggest he be 'deprived of diplomatic immunity'. What other corks may emerge from their pop-guns?

John Vestey
Porto Ercole, Grosseto, Italy

SIR – Broadcast on the ten o'clock news this evening was a film report which showed the Foreign Secretary retiring into his diplomatic car following his Libya meeting with the French President. William Hague duly proceeded to mark his briefing notes with a rather cheap-looking, blue ballpoint pen.

Even in a time of austere measures, I believe the Treasury could afford to provide him with a more superior writing tool for the job. I happen to have available a rather nice classic black and gold-finish Parker 51 vintage fountain pen, if the FCO is interested.

Andrew Porter
Harleston, Suffolk

SIR – The spending cuts must be having an effect at the BBC, as Huw Edwards hasn't presented the ten o'clock news from Libya yet.

Robin Easton
Bishop Auckland, Co. Durham

NO FLIES ON THE ARABS

SIR – If the Arab League is so keen on a no-fly zone over Libya why doesn't it take on the job? It has plenty of aircraft and an ideal base in Egypt. If the West is pushed into doing it, the virtuous aspects will soon be forgotten and the militants will list it as yet another 'assault on Islam'.

We delivered Muslims in Malaysia from Communist insurgency; rescued Muslims in Kuwait from aggression by Iraq; stopped ethnic cleansing of Muslims in the Balkans – all at the cost of British lives. We get precious few thanks now.

Brian Fish
Canterbury

SIR – A no-fly zone over Libya seems an excellent idea. The Libyans have enough problems without flies.

Ray Cantrell
Colchester, Essex

SIR – Surely the most effective means of ensuring the no-fly zone in Libya would be to bribe their baggage handlers to strike; it seems to work every summer in Spain.

Anthony Lord
Thornton-Cleveleys, Lancashire

SIR – From pictures of the Libyan uprising, I sense that none of this could happen without Toyota pick-up trucks.

When Tony Blair was last there did he not take a Land Rover salesman with him? Land Rovers are British and, unlike Toyotas or their manufacturers, have a long history of vehicular desert warfare in precisely that neck of the dunes.

Dirk H. R. Jones
Sonning Common, Oxfordshire

SIR – Has anyone else noted from the newsreels how pristine the Libyan road surfaces look compared to our pothole-ridden roads? It makes you think Gaddafi got one thing right.

Ronald Childs
Upminster, Essex

SIR – As Colonel Gaddafi declares an immediate ceasefire in response to the no-fly zone, he once more shows that he is not just a pretty face.

Tom Colborne-Malpas
London SW18

SIR – We are bombing Colonel Gaddafi because he is bombing his own people. Why can't he stick to bombing other people's people like the rest of us?

Trevor Wray
Stroud, Gloucestershire

MUAMMAR'S MODESTY

SIR – Gazing in wonder and admiration at the beribboned chest of Colonel Gaddafi, it occurred to me: how come this gallant guy never made General?

James Young
Burnham Market, Norfolk

SIR – Muammar Gaddafi was not a captain in 1964, as your correspondent claims. I was a member of the British Embassy in Libya in 1969. In September, when the revolution occurred, I was in Benghazi and by a quirk of geography the broadcasting station where Gaddafi set up his HQ was less than 100 yards from the Embassy office. I met him several times in the early days of the revolution.

He and the other eleven members of his Revolutionary Command Council came from the same graduating class at the military academy and were all due to be promoted captain in August 1969. However, Gaddafi and one other (Muhammad al-Magarief) were passed over because they were politically suspect.

On the day of the revolution, Gaddafi wore a lieutenant's insignia. He and the other officers then removed their badges of rank, but it was usually possible to infer what they had been by the pattern of the pinholes on their epaulettes.

When Gaddafi emerged as leader of the revolution he took the rank of colonel. In other words, he was never a captain at all.

Keith Haskell
Farringdon, Hampshire

SIR – Gaddafi has gone. Who is next? Assad in Syria? The real problem comes when the house of Saud is toppled – as it will, inevitably, be.

Peter Davies
Reading, Berkshire

SIR – I am sixty-three years old. I have never been involved in a street protest about anything, but if the British government decides to get involved in the war in Syria, I will take to the streets and throw a stone at somebody.

Neil Turner
Farnborough, Hampshire

FISH-AND-CHIP-EATING SURRENDER MONKEYS

SIR – It wasn't Cameron who was humiliated by the Syrian vote in the Commons, it was Great Britain. Who are the 'surrender monkeys' now? I feel ashamed to be British.

Godfrey Dann
East Grinstead, West Sussex

SIR – After a ten-year absence, will French fries be back on the menu in Washington?

Jack Melling
Salisbury, Wiltshire

SIR – Thank goodness Cameron and Miliband weren't around when the Argentines invaded the Falklands. Between them, they would have lost a Commons vote and let the Argentines secure their goal.

Watch out, Gibraltarians.

Brian Morgan
St Austell, Cornwall

SIR – By falsifying reasons for war to present to the British Parliament, the ex-Prime Minister, Tony Blair, is now additionally responsible for that same Parliament turning its back on the proven suffering of helpless women, men and children.

The main back-turners were from Labour, the party of Mr Blair's rancid government. What an appalling moment for British politics.

Patrick Ryecart
London SW10

SIR – Your correspondent Colonel Rayner points out that evil prospers while good men do nothing. He omits the supplementary, that it prospers even more when they do the wrong thing.

John Forrester
Edinburgh

SIR – David Cameron had an idea. That idea was rejected by the nation – in Parliament. This is something of which we may be hugely proud.

This is no humiliation but the essence of democracy at work. Let's have more of it.

Philip Hodson
Newmarket, Suffolk

SIR – The last time an RAF crew in an RAF aircraft was shot down in air-to-air combat was on 6 November 1956 – by a Syrian Air Force pilot in the same squadron as President Assad's father.

Downing Street might have forgotten this. The Syrian regime most certainly won't.

Andrew Brookes RAF (retd)
London SW9

BRING BACK BENIGN BASHAR

SIR – How the West must yearn for the return of the good old days of Hosni Mubarak, Saddam Hussein and Muammar Gaddafi. We do still have Bashar al-Assad, who now seems positively benign compared with the Islamic State.

Ian Macleod
Whitchurch, Shropshire

SIR — Harold Macmillan was a specialist in quips on the Arab world. His best, I thought, was after the toppling of Naguib by Nasser: 'No Middle Eastern ruler is so bad his successor cannot be worse.'

Denis Harvey-Kelly
Sherborne, Dorset

SIR — The Roman Valerius Maximus (first century AD) tells how an old woman prayed every day for the survival of the vicious tyrant of Syracuse, Dionysius. Dionysius heard about her and demanded to know why.

She replied: 'When I was a young girl, we used to have a severe tyrant, and wanted rid of him. But when he was killed, a much fiercer tyrant took over. Again, I thought it essential that his tyranny end. But now we have you, and you are even more oppressive than the others. So I keep offering my own life on behalf of your safety, because if you were removed, an even worse man would take your place.'

Valerius adds: 'Dionysius was too ashamed to punish her witty audacity.'

Jeannie Cohen, Peter Jones (Friends of Classics)
Newcastle upon Tyne

SIR — David Cameron says that this struggle will last the rest of his political lifetime. The Allies defeated the Nazis in six years. Surely if all the nations opposed to ISIL, including those in the Middle East, united together militarily under the auspices of the UN, they could get rid of it very quickly?

Anthony Gould
London W1

SIR – Could Tony Blair, winner of *GQ Magazine*'s 'philanthropist of the year' award, and special envoy for the Middle East Quartet, be dispatched to Iraq to deploy his much-vaunted abilities there?

J. H. Baines
Heckington, Lincolnshire

SIR – As a result of this crisis, when some British Muslims call for a caliphate under sharia law, we know what they mean.

C. M. Bartel
Orpington, Kent

SIR – Am I alone in repudiating the notion of a 'British jihadist'? Surely the terms are mutually exclusive.

Christopher Macy
Lincoln

SIR — Events in Syria, Iraq, Palestine and Ukraine are causing tremendous concern among political and religious leaders. Some events are truly horrifying. And what is the EU doing? It is banning vacuum cleaners over 1,600 watts.

Steve Cartridge
Bolton, Lancashire

PRINCE VS PUTIN

SIR — Vladimir Putin's aide accused the Prince of Wales of 'historical ignorance'. We all know that Prince Charles received a brilliant education.

As for President Putin, I have read all of his statements in newspapers and on television for the past twenty years, and found no sign of historical knowledge.

He presumably knows a little geography, however — of Crimea.

Oleg Gordievsky
London WC1

SIR — President Putin's aide is reported to have said that Britain was 'just a small island' and 'no one pays any attention to them'. Was David Cameron more annoyed that he said what he did, or that he is right? More to the point, what is he going to do about it?

Simon Roberts
Torquay, Devon

SIR — Teddy Roosevelt's dictum was to speak softly and carry a big stick. Now we see Barack Obama, David Cameron and William Hague speaking loudly and carrying feather dusters. Perhaps this is the true legacy of the nuclear age.

David Silber
Upton-upon-Severn, Worcestershire

SIR — Am I alone in thinking we should tell Vladimir Putin to stick his gas-pipe up his fundament and apply a lighted match to it?

M. E. Martin
Southborough, Kent

SIR — In 1968, while I was serving with the 1st British Corps in Germany, it became clear that divisions from the Group of Soviet Forces in Germany were moving towards the Czechoslovak frontiers.

I asked my commander whether steps should be taken to enhance the state of readiness by recalling personnel on leave or ensuring the tanks were ready for battle. He replied that no orders to that effect had been received through the NATO chain of command and that the regiment should carry on with normal peacetime training. So as we watched the dramatic events of the invasion of Czechoslovakia unfold, no specific action was taken.

Despite differences from the situation in Ukraine, and the longer distances, I can't help wondering if commanders of units in the NATO Rapid Reaction Corps, the headquarters of which is based in this country, are now asking similar questions and receiving a similar response.

Lt Gen Sir Richard Vickers
Dorchester

SIR – Despite David Cameron's protestations that the economic burden of EU sanctions against Russia should be spread across the bigger countries, it looks as if Britain is going to suffer a disproportionate hit to our financial services industry.

I'm reminded of the excellent seventies comedy *The Fall and Rise of Reginald Perrin*, wherein Reggie's boss would call to make an appointment. Reggie would reply that any time would be convenient, except two o'clock. Inevitably, Reggie always ended up agreeing to a two o'clock appointment.

Does this now typify our relationship with the EU?

Tom Jefferson
Howden, East Yorkshire

SIR — David Cameron said: 'There can be no excuse for outside military intervention in Ukraine — a point I made to President Putin when we spoke yesterday.'

This reminds me of Peter Sellers saying he was 'totally against the Second World War and wrote a letter saying so'. Sadly for Mr Cameron, Britain's global influence has been diluted by the emasculation of our Armed Forces, while our international political strength has been transferred enthusiastically to Brussels.

Peter Ferguson
Hertford

DECLINE AND FALL

SIR — As someone born in British India, I think David Cameron is inflating his ego greatly to imagine that Britain caused the world's problems. The British empire was a grand phase in world history while it lasted — just like so many other empires. Britons should be proud of its legacy, which allowed Indians smoothly to carry on governance after independence.

Mr Cameron seems to have caught Barack Obama's foolish bug of apologizing in order to ingratiate himself to other states at the expense of his own citizens.

Jiti Khanna
Vancouver, British Columbia, Canada

SIR – Mr Cameron seems very free and easy with his apologies of late. When will he apologize to the millions who voted for him thinking that he was a Conservative?

Mark Hudson
Smarden, Kent

SIR – It was brave of Mr Cameron to admit that Britain has caused many of the world's problems. However, by referring to historic events, Mr Cameron, intentionally or not, implies that Britain no longer plays a part in creating problems in the world.

Ian Johnson
Chelford, Cheshire

THE BIG SOCIETY ARMY

SIR – With the downgrading of our Armed Forces and the call for the Big Society, will the defence of the realm become the responsibility of Captain George Mainwaring and the rest of *Dad's Army*?

Josh Cosnett
Oxted, Surrey

SIR — With regard to the news of further cuts in defence spending, I don't know what effect they have on our enemies, but, by God, they frighten me.

Peter Davey
Bournemouth, Dorset

SIR — In 2009, the *Telegraph* printed a letter from me with the light-hearted suggestion that our stretched Armed Forces in Afghanistan should apply for overseas aid to balance their budget.

The suggestion was meant as a joke. Not anymore.

Brian Bullock
Doncaster, South Yorkshire

SIR — David Cameron is quite right to insist on the withdrawal of our troops from Afghanistan as soon as possible.

The English contingents must be deployed immediately in the Cheviots in preparation for the forthcoming Anglo-Scottish war over the sovereignty of Berwick-upon-Tweed.

Neil Bancroft
Christchurch, Dorset

7. Power of Scotland

THE AULD ENEMY

SIR — Boris Johnson's fairy-tale descriptions of holidays in the Scottish Highlands do not balance out the inequities of the Barnett Formula and the West Lothian question.

There has never been a special relationship between the two countries. The Romans built a wall and walked away, the Picts established their own nation, and throughout history war was a prevalent state of affairs. Scotland's 'Auld Alliance' was with France, not England.

The Act of Union was, from England's point of view, a way of ensuring that Scotland paid homage to the Crown, and Scotland was bankrupt and in need of support. A hundred years of sharing a monarch was the case of a 'single crown, but two countries'.

The Act was never a bringing together of kindred spirits.

Harry Maddock
Bristol

SIR — Having been dead set against independence for Scotland, I have recently changed my mind. It may cost the rest of the United Kingdom a few billion but it would open up the possibility of being able to deport George Galloway as an undesirable alien.

M. B.
Overton-on-Dee, Wrexham

SIR — Briefly, please. What is the point of Scotland?

John A. Jones
Sketty, Swansea

SIR — On 28 May 1929, Edinburgh celebrated the 600th anniversary of the granting of a charter by King Robert the Bruce. The principal event was the unveiling of the statues of Robert Bruce and William Wallace outside the entrance to Edinburgh Castle by the Duke of York (later to become King George VI).

He said that both he and the Duchess of York could claim descent from Bruce, and continued: 'Six hundred years have passed away, and these two countries, who were then the bitterest of foes, have become sister nations linked together by the closest bonds of blood and affection, bonds which have been cemented by the most enduring tie of all — comradeship in war.'

Scotland and England need each other.

Dr F. G. Anderson
Edinburgh

SIR — I look forward to an independent Scotland. It will put to bed that unease that an Englishman feels whenever he is described as a Briton.

Orlando Bridgeman
London W2

SIR – You report that David Cameron, on a British government trip to China, gave the Chinese President an England football strip. Is it any wonder foreigners see England and Britain as the same entity?

Alistair Leitch
Morpeth, Northumberland

SIR – After many years, our close friendship with a professional Scottish couple came under serious review when they invited my wife and me to a supper of haggis with boiled turnips. Until this incident, we had regarded them as quite cultured.

Raymond Barry
Laytham, East Yorkshire

ON THE NO-HOPE CAMPAIGN TRIAL

SIR – If I were a Scot, a visit from three no-hoper English politicians such as Messrs Cameron, Clegg and Miliband would drive me into the Yes camp immediately.

Dr Terry Langford
Milford on Sea, Hampshire

SIR – If Mr Cameron loses Scotland, he can console himself in having achieved same-sex marriage, a tax on plastic bags and a doubling of the national debt.

Brian Edmonds
Farnham, Surrey

SIR – Alex Salmond, the Scottish First Minister, will give those over the age of sixteen a vote in the referendum on independence.

Winston Churchill said that 'the greatest argument against democracy is a five-minute chat with the average voter'. I think we can all imagine what the great man would have thought after having a five-minute chat with the average sixteen-year-old voter.

Dr Andy Dyson
Southwell, Nottinghamshire

SIR – Alex Salmond has missed a golden opportunity for a decisive vote in favour of independence. He should have insisted the English take part in the referendum.

Chris Barmby
Tonbridge, Kent

SIR – Alex Salmond, Nicola Sturgeon? Something sounds a bit fishy to me.

Joan Campanini
Twickenham, Middlesex

SIR – If independence means less of Alex Salmond on our radio and television, bring it on.

Michael H. Peters
Sittingbourne, Kent

SIR – In this weekend's St Leger, the last classic horse race of the year, Alex My Boy came eighth of twelve runners, with Scotland coming last.

Tony Derbyshire
Sutton Coldfield, Warwickshire

SIR – Alex Salmond and the Yes camp seem to be dwelling on their discontent at being ruled by an out-of-touch government in London.

They may be surprised to find that this feeling is replicated all over the United Kingdom. My calling for an independent Leicestershire, however, is not the solution. We are far stronger if we stick together.

W. H. Statt
Snarestone, Leicestershire

SIR – In the eighteenth and nineteenth centuries Cornwall was a wealthy county producing tin, copper and other ores. At one stage 50,000 miners were working in Cornwall. Two-thirds of the entire copper production of the world came from Cornwall. Then the bottom fell out of the market, the ores were discovered in other countries, where they were more cheaply mined, and Cornwall declined to where it is now — one of the lowest-income areas in Great Britain.

Learn from our history, Scotland, and don't think your present source of wealth will last forever.

Anita Bowden

Harrowbarrow, Cornwall

SIR — As one who was based in Scotland during the unceasing efforts to counter the Soviet threat in the North Atlantic and Arctic oceans during the Cold War, any prospect of the northern defences of this island coming under the direction of pacifist Scottish Nationalists fills me with dread. This is especially so now that the Russian bear is again unsheathing its claws.

Sqn Ldr Seamus Hamill-Keays RAF (retd)

Llansantffraed, Breconshire

SIR — May I suggest that the government takes a leaf out of Putin's book and sends troops to Scottish cities to mingle with the citizens. This would reassure them that they are being protected from the possibility of becoming an independent state.

W. K. Wood

Bolton, Lancashire

CONUNDRUMS FOR THE DIVORCE LAWYERS

SIR – In all the talk about a referendum on Scottish independence there has been little mention of Scotland's share of the United Kingdom's national debt.

When the Labour government came to power in 1997, the national debt was around £350 billion. Shortly before Labour left office in 2010 it was forecasting a level of about £1,400 billion in 2015.

Scottish bankers played a disproportionately prominent role in reckless activity during the Labour years – the notion that banking excess is exclusive to London, a view common among Scots, needs to be vigorously opposed.

Under such circumstances, there can be no case for an independent Scotland taking on anything less than its fair share of the UK national debt.

Norman McChesney
Hawkhurst, Kent

SIR – When Scottish Nationalists divorce, do they retain their joint bank accounts?

Dr Andy Ashworth
Bo'ness, West Lothian

SIR – Please inform Mr Salmond that I have solved his currency problem: bitcoins.

Geoffrey Crabtree
Hucking, Kent

SIR – Alex Salmond announced on Wednesday that 'every man, woman and child would be £1,000 a year better off if Scotland became independent. That's £2,000 for every family.' Could he please give us a definition of a Scottish family and an explanation of the new maths he is employing?

James Barry
Stokesley, North Yorkshire

SIR – If the unthinkable happens, what of the Union flag? I see no reason to change it. After all, the flag shows our common heritage and that cannot change.

I doubt whether Australia, New Zealand, or indeed Hawaii, will modify their own national flags to reflect Scottish independence.

Professor M. M. R. Williams
Eastbourne, East Sussex

SIR – As an Englishman, I think it would be a backward step for Scotland to leave the Union, but if the Scots do decide to break away, please can we keep Carol Kirkwood?

Gordon Carter
Halesowen, West Midlands

SIR – Just a thought: if Scotland does achieve full independence, what will be left? Little Britain?

John Thorndycraft
Greenford, Middlesex

SIR – If Scotland votes for independence, will we in the rest of the UK be able to have British Summer Time all year?

Angela Bareford
Woking, Surrey

SIR – Would National Savings still be administered in Glasgow?

Peter Hull
Hoo, Kent

SIR – Which football league would Berwick Rangers play in?

Colin Walker
Lancaster

SIR – What will Nigel Farage call his party if there is no United Kingdom?

Ian Smee
Sutton Mandeville, Wiltshire

SIR – Presumably, everyone in Scotland would have to change email addresses to exclude reference to the UK.

Guy Mills
Chideock, Dorset

SIR – I have just sent Christmas cards to all my friends
and relatives in Scotland to avoid the possibility of paying
overseas postage.

Moira Brodie
Swindon, Wiltshire

SIR – One of your correspondents suggested that 'the zip
that is Hadrian's Wall can be undone', allowing Scotland
to drift off on its own.

Is he therefore suggesting that England cede
Northumberland and part of Cumbria to the Scots as a
parting gift?

David Hurrell
Alnwick, Northumberland

SIR – If Scotland says Yes, how quickly can we dump
Northern Ireland, Wales and Cornwall as well?

Robert Warner
Ramsbury, Wiltshire

A VICTORY FOR POLITENESS

SIR – The slogan for one side was 'No thanks' while the
other just had 'Yes' without the 'please'. Look who came
out on top.

Cate Goodwin
Easton-on-the-Hill, Northamptonshire

SIR – Scotland has spoken. May we now hope that it will shut up?

David Cole
Salisbury, Wiltshire

SIR – During the referendum campaign, life in Scotland has been unpleasant, divisive and upsetting. I pray that we never have to go through this again.

Rosemary Gould
St Andrews, Fife

SIR – Politicians keep telling me I want change. They are wrong.

Peter Washington
Presteigne, Radnorshire

SIR – How can we motivate 84 per cent of voters to turn out at the general election?

Drew Brooke-Mellor
Hastings, East Sussex

SIR – If David Cameron is guilty of such a breach of protocol as to pass on a private conversation with the Queen

('Cameron says Queen "purred" at Scotland result'), one can only wonder how many other unreported gaffes he makes at international conferences.

Kevin Heneghan
St Helens, Lancashire

SIR – My putative ancestor Robert Devereux, Earl of Essex, once got his ears boxed by Queen Elizabeth I. I hope this provides a suitable precedent when David Cameron apologizes to our present Queen for his recent 'purring' gaffe.

Tony Devereux
Theydon Bois, Essex

SIR – When David Cameron is kicked out by the Conservatives, I will positively purr.

Robert Hall
Skipton, North Yorkshire

SIR – As the SNP blames the BBC and everyone else for the referendum result, perhaps it should ponder a piece of betting-shop lore that has been the salvation of many gamblers. If you make excuses for beaten horses, you'll end up living in a cardboard box.

Michael Stanford
London SE23

8. Anti-Social Media

A SHORTLIST OF TRUSTWORTHIES

SIR – The hacking scandal left my family debating who we can still rely on. Our shortlist of trustworthies came down to the Gurkhas, other ranks in our Armed Forces, postmen and Simon the pieman, who works in the butcher's shop.

Garry May

Haddenham, Buckinghamshire

SIR – As a banker, is it safe to come out now?

Andrew Holgate

Woodley, Cheshire

SIR – My late father was a journalist on the *Daily Mirror* from the 1970s to the 1990s. He opted out after Maxwell appeared. In his retirement, he said: 'Editors today are paid to make people do what I used to be paid to stop people doing.'

David Keates

Grundisburgh, Suffolk

SIR – Over the last century, in books and films, the perception of the newspaper editor has been of an all-knowing individual with complete control over every journalist and every story related to his or her newspaper, including the journalistic methods employed.

However, we now know that, in the case of Mrs Brooks, she appeared to display such hands-off leadership that one must wonder why she was employed in such a role. I can only assume she had hidden talents.

Christopher Devine
Farley, Wiltshire

SIR – Try as I might to concentrate on Rebekah Brooks's possible wrongdoings, all I can think about is the impossibility of getting a comb through that hair.

Doraine Potts
Woodmancote, Gloucestershire

SIR – At last it has emerged that 'Mr Cameron probably rode the horse more than Mrs Brooks'. One is bound to ask, therefore: how often did he ride Mrs Brooks?

David Townson
Isleworth, Middlesex

THE END OF THE WORLD

SIR – In the penultimate edition of the *News of the World*, did the resident astrologer predict the demise of the paper? If not – why not?

Dr Bob Turvey
Bristol

SIR — How brave of the Murdoch empire to leave the *News of the World* sinking ship at such an appropriate moment. May we expect to see a replacement rag?

John Breining-Riches
Chagford, Devon

SIR — As an incurably forgetful person with no experience of running a multinational corporation, I feel I am more than qualified to replace James Murdoch. In fact, I already have no recollection of submitting my application later today.

Dominic Pike
Edinburgh

SIR — Should one trust a man whose pocket handkerchief is made from the same material as his shirt? I only ask because this strange affectation was being displayed by James Murdoch last week.

Simon Baumgartner
Hampton, Middlesex

SIR — I was trying to think who Rupert Murdoch and his son reminded me of, then it came to me: Montgomery Burns and his sidekick Smithers in *The Simpsons*.

Peter Sanders
Bishops Waltham, Hampshire

SIR – All the Australians I have asked about the greatest living Australian have responded: 'He's American.'

Alex Henney
London N6

SIR – I watched two Tom Watsons on television this week. I now know why I prefer golf to politics.

Clive Allen
Draycote, Warwickshire

THE REAL LEVESON INQUIRY

SIR – I wonder if the good Lord Leveson would mind taking a short break from his exacting task to make a judicial statement about the correct pronunciation of his name. Opinion seems to be divided pretty well 50/50 as to whether the *eve* bit is as in 'Adam and Eve' or as in 'heavenly'.

The suspense of waiting to hear which option the next speaker will select is beginning to get on my wick.

Margaret Kimberley
West Mersea, Essex

SIR – I'm baffled: how do Cabinet ministers have the time to send so many texts and emails? Do they dictate them to a civil servant? Or do they use predictive text or shorthand, such as 'gr8 news Rup'?

Ian Henderson
Witney, Oxfordshire

SIR – Email is used to discuss matters which, in a properly structured letter, would never be said or sent.

The immediacy and ease of email enables that which should not be said to become a permanent record. With more thought and less finger-stabbing, many of these ills would not arise.

James Bishop
Wincanton, Somerset

SIR – I find myself in an impossible situation – after Wednesday's Leveson Inquiry hearings, am I to believe Gordon Brown or Rupert Murdoch?

Julia Brotherton
Chippenham, Wiltshire

SIR – Try as I will, I cannot feel sympathy for Gordon Brown on learning that he may have had details of his bank account obtained. While in office, he had no concern about obtaining as much information as he could about my account and then extracting a large portion of it.

Peter Gee
Ellesmere, Shropshire

SIR – I hope the Leveson Inquiry ends soon; I've had more than enough of photos of Jeremy Hunt and his bicycle.

Edward Huxley
Thorpe, Surrey

SIR – I hope that Jeremy Hunt is not taking too much comfort from the fact that David Cameron has announced that Mr Hunt has his full support and confidence.

Over the past few decades in British politics, the time between a prime minister voicing his support and that person being sacked or resigning has been approximately two to three weeks.

Robert Readman
West Bournemouth, Dorset

SIR – Perhaps James Naughtie was right, after all.

Robert Dobson
Seal, Kent

TO REGULATE OR NOT TO
REGULATE

SIR – Lord Justice Leveson tells us that his proposed scheme 'is not, and cannot be characterized as, statutory regulation of the press'. He then suggests that (a) all those providing news should be asked to join a body with a power to fine them for breach of its code of practice; (b) that to ensure that compliance is not a matter of choice, any provider who refuses to join should be regulated willy-nilly by a 'backstop regulator' in the shape of Ofcom, with a similar power to fine for breaches of the code; and that (c) the requirements of the code should go considerably beyond the requirements of the law that affects the rest of us, embracing such matters as accuracy and alleged imbalance, with a right for pressure groups to complain and demand redress.

If this is not a proposal for the regulation of the press by statute, I would love to know what is.

Andrew Tettenborn, Professor of Commercial Law
Swansea University

SIR – I was taught by my A level Politics teacher that a free and unfettered press is essential to preserve democracy and hold a government to account. Was he wrong?

Louis Pakarian
Lancing, West Sussex

SIR – Voltaire apologized to a friend that he had no time to make his letter shorter. Lord Justice Leveson's 2,000-page report needs an editor to pull out the key issues. John Milton's *Areopagitica* remains the best summary of the issues involved with licensing the press and is much shorter. Judges and lawyers sometimes measure their worth by quantity rather than quality.

Ian Walker

Riddlesdown, Surrey

SIR – Alastair Campbell has told the Leveson Inquiry of his commitment to a free press. Is this the same Alastair Campbell who, when I was programme editor of the *Early Evening News* at ITN, tried to put the frighteners on the editorial executives to prevent us leading on the outcome of the O. J. Simpson trial instead of a speech by Tony Blair?

We stuck to our guns and earned some praise. The BBC led with Tony Blair.

Philip Moger

East Preston, West Sussex

SIR – Nick Clegg Liberal? Democratic? In his desire for legislative control of the press he disowns those credentials.

David Broughton

Woodborough, Wiltshire

SIR – Most rational people would happily accept a law that prohibited newspapers from mentioning, in any context, Hugh Grant, Steve Coogan and Charlotte Church.

Michael Stanford
London SE23

SIR – David Cameron says that we have managed without press regulation for 300 years. But we have not had telephones for that length of time, or the technology for hacking them.

He is wrong. The sleazy aspects of the press need to be controlled. Mr Cameron has friends in the sleazy part of the press, but he must surely see where his duty lies.

Ellis Field
York

THE WAGES OF SPIN

SIR – One of the most depressing things about the Coulson affair is that senior politicians seem desperate to appoint so-called spin doctors to explain their actions to the electorate. One cannot imagine Attlee or Churchill requiring such people around them.

The concept of just telling the truth is clearly beyond the understanding of the modern political class.

Colin Bullen
Tonbridge, Kent

SIR — 'Will Andy Coulson be for David Cameron what Christine Keeler was for Harold Macmillan?' asks Andrew Gilligan. If so, Mr Cameron has little to worry about.

Macmillan's fortunes revived quickly in the aftermath of the Profumo scandal, with a sharp rise in the opinion polls. At the start of October 1963 he made clear to Cabinet colleagues that he was staying on.

As D. R. Thorpe put it in his recent, brilliant biography *Supermac*, 'Macmillan was not brought down by Profumo; he was brought down by his prostate.'

Lord Lexden
London SW1

SIR — When John Profumo resigned his seat in March 1963, having admitted lying to Parliament, Iain Macleod, then Leader of the Commons, said: 'Jack Profumo was a friend of mine, is a friend of mine and will continue to be a friend of mine.'

I have always thought standing by friends, no matter what, is rare — especially in politics — and David Cameron rises in my estimation for standing by Andy Coulson.

Tom Benyon
Bladon, Oxfordshire

SIR — Your correspondent asks whether the hacking scandal is David Cameron's Laura Spence moment.

The closest parallel is with the Westland affair of 1985/6, when a relatively minor political problem was blown out of all proportion by the media and Labour Opposition, calling into question the integrity of the Prime Minister. For the record, Margaret Thatcher went on to win the next election only sixteen months later, with a majority of 102 seats.

Philip Duly
Haslemere, Surrey

SIR – I feel that David Cameron has chosen the wrong job. With so many of his friends, Cabinet members, press secretaries and old school chums facing prosecution, he should have been a lawyer and helped them in their time of need.

Derek Hanlin
Gilfach Goch, Rhondda

9. Chillaxing Conservatives

THE BULLINGDON BOYS

SIR — The Leader of the House of Lords, Thomas Galloway Dunlop du Roy de Blicquy Galbraith, 2nd Baron Strathclyde, claims that the Conservatives are not the rich, posh party. Indeed, how would he know?

Jack Woodford
Buckfastleigh, Devon

SIR — If Ed Miliband refers to David Cameron and his Cabinet as 'posh boys', is it politically correct to refer to Mr Miliband and his gang as 'plebs'?

Craig Kennedy
Brookfield, Renfrewshire

SIR — The word 'posh' as used in relation to the Conservative Party is merely a Labour weapon in its politics of envy, but it is dangerous nevertheless.

Winston Churchill, a scion of the Marlboroughs, was never described as posh. He was able to walk with kings, yet keep the common touch. Perhaps there is a lesson there.

Alec Ellis
Liverpool

SIR — It was Tony Benn who, when accused of being out of touch with the common man, given his upbringing as the heir to Viscount Stansgate, and his wife's wealth, replied: 'A doctor does not have to be ill to treat his patients successfully.'

Rather annoyingly, in this case I agree with the old Leftie.

Ben Howkins
Staverton, Devon

SIR — There can be no better example of how out of touch this government is than George Osborne's constant use of the dropped 't' and the glottal stop — a wholly unconvincing attempt to ingratiate himself with the masses. In this mixed, but essentially Conservative, part of East Kent, I have never heard anyone speak as he does.

Elizabeth Weston
Sandwich, Kent

SIR — David Davis betrays a disappointing chippiness with his criticisms of the public-school clique at the heart of government.

The public had no problem engaging with Boris Johnson (Eton) or with Nigel Farage (Dulwich), let alone Tony Blair, the Fettes boy who so devastatingly humbled the pre-Cameron Tory Party.

John Rees
London W14

SIR – Tuesday's *Daily Telegraph* front page featured four Old Etonians – Boris and Leo Johnson, Prince Harry and David Cameron.

I have nothing but sympathy for their mutually endured affliction and have several friends who continue to suffer in the same way, but did anything of consequence happen to people who did not attend Eton's hallowed halls?

Gareth Pryce
Hayling Island, Hampshire

SIR – When David Cameron became leader of the Conservative Party, I wondered whether he had any strong political principles and ambitions other than becoming Prime Minister.

I have been reading Lord Owen's excellent book *In Sickness and in Power*, and was struck by his comment about another Old Etonian prime minister, Harold Macmillan: 'Although he had a fine intellect, he was a classic example of an actor politician; not for nothing was he sometimes called the "Old Poseur".'

Is history repeating itself?

Dr Brian Cooper
Bromsgrove, Worcestershire

SIR – Your leading article refers to David Cameron's 'great personal charm'. I would suggest that this is the last quality we should look for in a politician, as it is the major attribute of all successful con men.

Angus McPherson
Findon, West Sussex

DANISH PATSY

SIR – Could it be that in appearing to be flirting with Helle Thorning-Schmidt, the glamorous Danish Prime Minister, at Nelson Mandela's memorial service, David Cameron was actually lobbying for a cameo role in *Borgen*?

Gerald Fisher
Kettering, Northamptonshire

LAST AMONG EQUALS

SIR – Mr Bercow declares: 'All Are Equal.' I don't think so – I couldn't afford £37,000 for a portrait of myself.

Alan Lyall
Weston-super-Mare, Somerset

SIR – The ladder on Mr Bercow's coat of arms is to mark his rise to the top. I had assumed that it represented an essential accoutrement to kiss his wife.

Graham Masterton
Tadworth Park, Surrey

SIR – Sally Bercow, the wife of the Speaker, admits to a drunken ladette past by drinking a whole bottle of wine a day, maybe even two. SHOCK! HORROR!

Dear Sally, a word to the wise: consuming two bottles of wine a day does not make you a drunk; it makes you a passable companion for dinner. Two bottles of vodka, you're getting there. Two bottles of vodka and bottles of wine for chasers, you're definitely getting there.

You were not a ladette, dear Sally. You were a poor wino, and barely an accomplished one at that.

Albert Roy
London E3

SIR – I looked at the shelf of books behind the Speaker's wife, in the photograph on your front page yesterday.

I can understand the biographies of Churchill (two), Nixon, William Hague, Betty Boothroyd and Cherie Blair, but I am slightly worried about that of Pol Pot.

Dr Martin Henry
Good Easter, Essex

SIR – With the revelations about their private lives, it is about time John Bercow and his wife starred in a new film called *Carry on Commons*.

It would have all the ingredients for success: a beautiful leggy blonde and a sexually frustrated little man brought together by a desire to make their fortune.

Ted Shorter
Hildenborough, Kent

SIR – John Bercow's delivery of his 'kaleidoscope' speech in front of the Queen was worthy of Jane Austen's Mr Collins. Should the BBC ever be tempted to commission another adaptation of *Pride and Prejudice*, that's one piece of casting taken care of.

Mark Shirley
London SW6

SIR – Bercow by name, Bercow by nature. Give him a bit part in the next *Game of Thrones*.

N. P. Scott
Harpenden, Hertfordshire

MINUS ONE FOR THE ROAD

SIR — My sympathies go out to the Prime Minister, who accidentally left his daughter at a public house.

Several years ago, my seven-year-old son went missing at Tesco. I left my wife, son and daughter to return home and start cooking supper. When I heard the family return, my wife called out 'James'. I asked her reason. She replied: 'Because he returned with you.'

'No he didn't,' I said. 'I left him with you.'

A hurried telephone call put our minds at rest. He was busy tucking into fish and chips in the staff canteen.

John Barker
Prestbury, Cheshire

SIR — David and Samantha Cameron are not the first couple to make such an omission.

Our Lord Jesus was left behind in the temple at Jerusalem for three days, when Joseph and Mary returned home after the feast of Passover (Luke 2:5).

John Barrie
Purley, Surrey

SIR — Far worse than leaving the kids in the pub is my experience of having my kids leave me in the pub.

Doug Humphreys
Shirley, Surrey

SIR – Should we be pleased to know that the Prime Minister's security team are so single-minded that they concentrate only on Mr Cameron, or concerned that they too can't count?

Bernard Kerrison
London SW4

SIR – May I suggest that the next time David and Samantha Cameron go out for a Sunday pub lunch they take Nick Clegg, the Deputy Prime Minister, but do not return to find him.

Roger Redfarn
Westbourne, West Sussex

THE JOY OF CHILLAXING

SIR – I note that David Cameron is 'chillaxing'. Does the presence of this monstrous word on the front page of the *Daily Telegraph* mean that it has now moved to common use? Or is there a subliminal message that Mr Cameron is turning into a chilling axe man, as many would have us believe?

Stuart Taylor
Oxford

SIR – Chillaxing is nothing new among prime ministers. Winston Churchill painted landscapes and built a wall. Margaret Thatcher holidayed by the sea. John Major watched the cricket. Tony Blair time-shared with Sir Cliff Richard. David Cameron watches DVDs and has a glass of wine.

However, Gordon Brown chewed his fingernails and lost a general election.

Anthony Rodriguez
Staines-upon-Thames, Middlesex

RIP, THE IRON LADY

SIR – I'll say one thing for Margaret Thatcher: unlike Blair or Cameron, she could always be relied upon to stab you in the front.

Mike Wright
Nuneaton, Warwickshire

SIR – Modern political leaders crave our love: it is their weakness. Margaret Thatcher did not set out to be loved – or even to be liked. This was her strength, and she won more respect than any of her successors have done.

Richard Tracey
Dinan, Côtes-d'Armor, France

SIR – I am bitterly disappointed; I had presumed that she was immortal.

Charles Holcombe
Brighton

SIR – One of the great things about Margaret Thatcher as a politician was her command of good plain English. Even if people disagreed with her they knew why.

Ted Shorter
Tonbridge, Kent

SIR – In all the analysis of Lady Thatcher's political and personal attributes, I feel that one important item has been overlooked: her Christian name.

I have never met a Margaret who did not know who she was, where she was, where she was going and what she was going to do when she got there.

Capt Kim Mockett (husband of Mrs Margaret Mockett)
Littlebourne, Kent

SIR – Hearing of the sad death of Lady Thatcher reminded me that, for many years, my wife displayed on her desk at work a cutting from your newspaper: 'Behind every great woman is a Denis'.

Denis Graves
Crowborough, East Sussex

SIR – After I lost my seat in Parliament, I attended a dinner for Conservative MPs at which Denis Thatcher was the chief guest.

After the meal I found myself alone with him in the Gents and suggested that Mrs Thatcher should remember that when prime ministers are doing well they take the credit, so when there are problems they must expect to take the blame. He agreed.

I followed this up with the suggestion that if, after her tenth anniversary in office, she ceased to be Prime Minister she would go out in a blaze of glory, but if she stayed on – 'Who knows?'

He replied: 'I agree. But you tell her.'

Charles Simeons
Cley, Norfolk

SIR – Three or four years ago, as a treat, my husband and I had lunch at the Ritz. We spotted Margaret Thatcher and some friends at a secluded table. The feeling we experienced was the same as long ago seeing one's headmistress out of school.

Patricia Davies
Denmead, Hampshire

SIR – The world was a better place when Pope John Paul II, President Ronald Reagan and Margaret Thatcher were working together. It has been straight downhill for freedom since their departure from office.

Jane Trammell
Peachtree City, Georgia, United States

SIR – In the 1970s, in a small village market in Yugoslavia, the local lad running the vegetable stall was bemoaning in broken English the fact that they had rampant inflation.

I said to him: 'What you need is Margaret Thatcher.'

Quick as a flash, he said: 'No, what I need is Samantha Fox.'

Carole Buchanan
Wadebridge, Cornwall

SIR – To those of us who sailed to war in the South Atlantic in 1982, Margaret Thatcher gave clear, firm leadership.

When hostilities ceased and my battalion's second-in-command, Major Bill Dawson, told the world that a white flag was flying over Port Stanley, he concluded with a chuckle and the words, 'Bloody marvellous!' It was a term that might have applied to the Iron Lady herself.

Major Nigel Price
Marple Bridge, Cheshire

SIR – At the end of the miners' strike my husband's workplace was about to close. Two weeks short of completing a further year in the industry, with resulting loss of a year's pension rights, he was told by the management that it was just his bad luck.

A letter to Margaret Thatcher brought a rapid,

personal response, requesting the management to allow him to work a further two weeks.

She was a caring prime minister.

Josephine Fleming
Ashton-in-Makerfield, Lancashire

SIR – I hope those on the Left who may, unattractively, feel some jubilation at Lady Thatcher's death remember that she destroyed the hereditary power of the well-to-do, as well as that of the shop steward. She created a society where anyone could aim for the stars, regardless of the bed they were born in or the job their father had. This is her greatest legacy.

Charles Leggatt
Grantham, Lincolnshire

SIR – Lady Thatcher's funeral service began with a quotation from T. S. Eliot's *Four Quartets*. Perhaps an extract from *The Waste Land* would have been more appropriate.

P. D. J. MacGregor
Nickley Wood, Kent

SIR – Amid all the controversy, I think I can hear a clear, forceful voice: 'I'm enjoying this!'

I. P. F. Meiklejohn
Forres, Moray

SIR – Her statue, complete with handbag, should stand on a high plinth at the entrance to Downing Street, facing towards Europe.

Garry May
Haddenham, Buckinghamshire

SAMCAM 'N' DAVE

SIR – While it is welcome to see the vivacious Samantha Cameron and read about her support for her husband, why does she refer to him as 'Dave'? This is so degrading. It makes him sound like an odd-job man. We don't hear about Nic Sarkozy or Ange Merkel.

David Hartridge
Groby, Leicestershire

SIR – Why do our politicians feel the need to hold the hand of their spouse when attending state occasions? It is completely inappropriate. Why can't they follow the example of the Royal Family?

June Boyd
Carlisle

SIR – Why were Michelle Obama and Samantha Cameron, two educated women with impressive career experience outside the home, photographed sitting in pretty dresses, their hands folded neatly in their laps, in the Downing

Street kitchen? Yes, kitchens are important. Domestic life is important. Being a wife and mother is important. But women have fought for generations to escape being relegated to this role alone.

It's 2011. Women who marry men who go into politics should not be repackaged as 1950s magazine advertisements, forced to pretend that they're Stepford wives for the sake of their husbands' careers.

Anne Thackray
Toronto, Ontario, Canada

SIR – Samantha Cameron was shown wearing the same frock at the weekend that she wore at a party last week. This morning I am wearing my red skirt. I got it just after my son was born.

He is forty.

Patricia Lister
Whitby, North Yorkshire

SIR – In today's paper there was a photo of the Prime Minister on a night off, visiting a restaurant in a navy anorak and jeans. Could you imagine Harold Macmillan ever appearing on the streets of the capital dressed in this shabby way?

I will not vote for him again.

Barry Carroll
London SW4

SIR – It was enlightening to read that David Cameron hires his white tie and tails. It was not, however, entirely surprising. The Prime Minister suffers from a malady common among the wealthy, which causes them to disregard the rules of formal dress.

Despite possessing the means to have evening dress tailored, Mr Cameron insists on appearing at state banquets looking as though he is wearing someone else's waistcoat. Etiquette dictates it ought not extend below the flaps of the tailcoat, but Mr Cameron's does so by three inches.

Mitt Romney, the presidential candidate, displayed the same wardrobe malfunction at the Waldorf Astoria last week.

Paul Nizinskyj (Founder, The White Tie Club)
Sheffield

SIR – I have long been surprised at the clothing worn by the Prime Minister and his wife when running. David Cameron favours a cotton polo shirt and trainers, not running shoes, whereas Samantha appears to be taking part in a polar trek in assorted shirts and fleeces.

Any runner would advise proper running shoes and a breathable top.

Michael Powell
Tealby, Lincolnshire

SIR – David Cameron was almost knocked over by a jogger. While holidaying in the Isles of Scilly in the sixties, my girlfriend and I were walking to our hotel when there was a power cut. Struggling through the dark and crowded street, I cannoned into a man: we each offered our apologies and went on our way. My girlfriend then pointed out that it was Harold Wilson, the Prime Minister, that I had almost knocked down.

He and his wife owned a house there and consequently were frequent visitors. In those days there were no security guards in attendance, and he could often be seen walking alone on the beaches with his dog.

David Partington
Higher Walton, Warrington

#RESIGNED

SIR – All is well with the world. Sepp Blatter is in charge of FIFA, Bernie Ecclestone returns to Formula 1 and Baroness Warsi resigns over Gaza on Twitter before she tells the Prime Minister.

Martin Greenwood
Fringford, Oxfordshire

SIR – Of course Brooks Newmark had to resign: he wears paisley pyjamas.

Robert Warner
Ramsbury, Wiltshire

SIR – Is it not odd, and a trifle spooky, that the two Tory ministers whom Labour have gone after are Fox and Hunt? What can it mean?

Nicholas Guitard
Poundstock, Cornwall

SIR – Dr Fox was my GP some years ago, and on one occasion had to examine my nether regions. I am pleased to report that Adam Werritty was not present at the time.

Dr Martin Wheeley
Breedon on the Hill, Leicestershire

SIR – Dr Fox's performance in the Commons on Monday reminded me of Churchill's saying: 'He occasionally stumbled over the truth, but hastily picked himself up and hurried on as if nothing had happened.'

Len Stanley
Leigh-on-Sea, Essex

SIR – Surely it is time the electorate was given a mechanism for recalling MPs? Perhaps, in this electronic age, there could be an annual vote of confidence in MPs, with a significant dissatisfaction level leading to a by-election.

Ian Brown
Derby

THE MINISTER FOR INEQUALITY

SIR — I was relieved to hear of Maria Miller's resignation from the Cabinet, not a moment too soon. But does this limited action indicate that she considers her behaviour is acceptable for a backbench MP?

Ray Melvin
Bury St Edmunds, Suffolk

SIR — Before ministers are appointed to the Cabinet, they should be required to sit a short intelligence test: I. You have two homes and spend more nights each year in one than the other. Which one is your main home? 2. Can you recognize whether your parents are also living in one of your homes?

Guy Smith
Reigate, Surrey

SIR — We are constantly being told that we live in a 'compensation culture', driven by arrogance, greed and self-interest.

On reflection, perhaps Mrs Miller is indeed the best choice for the post of Culture Secretary.

Mick Richards
Llanfair Waterdine, Shropshire

SIR – Why do we need a Department for Culture, Media and Sport anyway? Why can't culture, media and sport just be left to get on with it?

Graham Read
Esher, Surrey

SIR – Why are wrongful expenses claims by MPs 'mistakes' but wrongful benefit claims classed as crimes?

Roy Parks
Llanymynech, Montgomeryshire

SIR – Now we know what David Cameron meant by: 'We are all in this together.'

Peter Leatherbarrow
Wortwell, Norfolk

SIR – If Samantha Cameron can earn £400,000 as a company director and yet the Prime Minister earns a relatively shabby £142,500 for running the country, why does it surprise people that politicians are on the fiddle and the House of Commons is full of people from privileged backgrounds?

Patricia Hall
Whittle-le-Woods, Lancashire

GOING IN TO BAT FOR HAGUE

SIR — William Hague and Christopher Myers shared a room when campaigning during the last election. So what? During the Himbleton Village Cricket team tour of Barnstaple, April 2009, I shared a room with Martyn Preece. However, that didn't mean we both batted for the other side.

Ben Sinclair
Bentley, Worcestershire

SIR — I shared a room with forty-nine other males when I was at school; it was called a dormitory.

Anthony Messenger
Windsor, Berkshire

SIR — As a conscript I shared my 'bedroom' with twenty-seven other young men. Was the war won by an army of homosexuals?

R. Edgar Jones
Penrhyn Bay, Conwy

SIR — It is not the allegations surrounding William Hague and his special adviser that I find extraordinary, but the fact that it is felt that the twenty-five-year-old Chris Myers, on a salary of £30,000, has any useful advice to offer the Foreign Secretary.

At twenty-five I was in no position to offer a Secretary of State any advice of any worth. Now at the age of fifty-one I feel I have a number of pieces of advice for any Cabinet ministers who would wish to listen. These are not, however, printable in the letters page of a leading daily newspaper.

S. P.
Headcorn, Kent

SIR – I presume there have never been any rumours that Tony Blair and Gordon Brown shared a hotel bedroom.

Ivor Yeloff
Norwich

I PRO*TEST* ABOUT CAMERON'S LANGUAGE

SIR – On the news a few months ago I heard David Cameron say 'I intend to transfer.' He put the stress on the first syllable of each verb. It is the noun which takes the stress on the first syllable, while the verb takes it on the second. This is the case with many words used as both nouns and verbs: contract, increase, survey and protest.

Churchill was gloriously aware of the rhythms, beauty and power of the English language. If Cameron wishes to emulate him, he needs to look to the quality and delivery of his English.

James MacDonald
Oundle, Peterborough

SIR – With reference to the fuss about David Cameron's remark 'Calm down, dear', I must say I quite enjoy familiar greetings in shops.

However, such greetings can mislead. My daughter told me of sitting in a pub in Derbyshire when a middle-aged couple, obviously not locals, walked in. The lady enquired: 'Are you serving sandwiches?'

The barman responded: 'Yes, duck.'

The lady then turned to her husband and said: 'Oh, I don't fancy duck.' So they left.

Dr Tony Hart
Sedgley, Staffordshire

DETOXIFYING THE BRAND

SIR – Can David Cameron explain to us the point of a modern and detoxified Conservative Party that is devoid of members?

Paul Elswood
Bursledon, Hampshire

SIR – Janet Daley writes about the political urge to occupy the centre ground. This reminds me of the 'ice-cream van' theory, whereby two ice-cream vans on a beach have to position themselves next to each other at the midpoint of the beach in order to deny as much territory as possible to the competition.

At the time it seemed to me that there was a danger of holidaymakers deciding that it was not worth the trek to the van for an ice cream. Now another van has set up closer to us.

Peter Gregory
Wotton-under-Edge, Gloucestershire

SIR – Your correspondent compares our leaders to cheeses, but says he has failed to think of something suitable for David Cameron. How about Stilton: blue, but only in part.

Dr Maurice Dixson
Kington Langley, Wiltshire

SIR – A suitable cheese with which to compare David Cameron is the square, flat, processed-plastic stuff.

We're told it's cheese – indeed it looks a little like cheese – but it is only pretending to be cheese, tastes nothing like cheese, and is a big disappointment.

Fiona Harper
Midgham, West Berkshire

SIR – David Cameron says that the Conservative Party should not 'tack this way, tack that way', but, as any sailor will tell you, that is the only way to make progress against a headwind.

What does not work is what he seems to be doing now, namely pointing head into wind, with the sails flapping, half the crew questioning the competence of the captain, and the rest of the fleet sailing on past.

Miles Williamson-Noble
Stamford, Lincolnshire

SIR – I'm still not sure if David Cameron 'gets it', but it certainly looks like he's got it coming.

Martyn Pitt
Hardwicke, Gloucestershire

SIR – In 2015 I am due to deliver 3,000 leaflets across my rural area in support of the re-election of my well-regarded local MP, John Glen.

Perhaps Mr Cameron could persuade one of his smart young metropolitan friends to come down to the shires to deliver on my behalf? They will require a pair of stout shoes and an umbrella.

Christopher Devine
Farley, Wiltshire

SIR – Grassroots party members do not win elections; the electorate at large chooses the government.

Loyal supporters as we are – we pay our subs, deliver leaflets, canvass, attend functions – I'm afraid that we are not so important, when compared with the electorate.

For example: I strongly oppose the concept of gay marriage, but I have to accept the evidence that the majority of the people under the age of forty, perhaps even fifty, support it.

We old codgers may be wise, experienced and correct but we are not in tune with the times.

I believe that Mr Cameron is more in touch with the zeitgeist than we are and, certainly, he is more respected by the electorate than the Labour leader is.

Disillusioned ex-Conservatives who seem disposed to vote for UKIP in 2015 should be aware that to do so is effectively to vote Labour – so our next prime minister will be Ed Miliband. The result will be no benefit for UKIP and disaster for Britain.

Keith B. Pearson
Whyteleafe, Surrey

SIR – David Cameron has tried to ease the pain of his party's local elections by renewing his vows with Nick Clegg in the relaunch of their beloved coalition government. In sharp contrast, Boris Johnson defied the national anti-Coalition vote and won the London mayoralty by standing for clear Conservative policies. David Cameron should do the same.

David Saunders
Sidmouth, Devon

BORIS FOR DONCASTER NORTH

SIR – As Boris is the Tories' greatest asset, why find him a safe seat? If they want to win the next election, they should put him up against Miliband, Balls or Clegg.

Brian Christley
Abergele, Denbighshire

SIR – My wife said something was up a fortnight ago, when Boris Johnson had his hair cut.

Geoff Chessum
London EC2

SIR – I have waited for years for something on which I can agree with Boris Johnson and at last, in his call to amalgamate thousands of public-sector pensions, it has arrived. Is this to be the start of something, like the cluster of London buses on the same route, or just a splendid one-off?

Richard Forth
Tunbridge Wells, Kent

SIR – May I suggest that it would save a great deal of faffing about if Boris Johnson stopped being so self-effacing and contested the seat for Witney, Oxfordshire, at the forthcoming general election.

That course of action, together with a firm pact with UKIP, is the only hope the Tories have.

Lance Warrington
Northleach, Gloucestershire

10. Swivel-eyed Loons

THE ARRIVAL OF FOUR-PARTY POLITICS

SIR – The dramatic entry of UKIP means that the cake will have to be split four ways now (assuming the Lib Dems don't become extinct). The shares look to be evenly divided among the biggest three, which can only mean that Britain faces a long future of coalition governments.

My hunch is that Nigel Farage will become Deputy Prime Minister in 2015.

Roger Brown
Dunholme, Lincolnshire

SIR – May I propose a 'farage' to mean a distant prospect that appears credible, but evaporates as the election grows nearer?

Ian McKenzie
Lincoln

SIR – Is there a chance that if Nigel Farage gets in, we might be able to smoke in pubs and drink affordable beer again?

Martin Thurston
Liphook, Hampshire

SIR – The Malay word for vagina is *faraj*, pronounced *farage*. As he is full of wind, he could have two rude nicknames.

John Evans
Buxted, East Sussex

WHY I'M VOTING UKIP . . .

SIR – During the televised EU debate, Nick Clegg accused Nigel Farage of wanting to turn back the clock and see W. G. Grace opening the batting for England.

I'm voting UKIP.

Bernard Anghelides
Paddock Wood, Kent

SIR – Your leading article does not mention the fundamental reason why many people like me, a former activist and Conservative voter in every election since 1979, will be voting UKIP. The Conservative Party, under the leadership of David Cameron, is no longer conservative.

It is now a party of uncontrolled, mass immigration into Britain. It is anti-family, penalizing those who wish, by choice, to stay at home and bring up their children. It believes in borrowing money at excessive levels in order to fund a deliberately ballooning overseas aid budget. It no longer advocates the effective security and defence of the realm as it continues to undermine the effectiveness of our Armed Forces. And it seems perfectly happy to build over our beautiful countryside, where once it represented a philosophical position that 'conserved what is good'.

The party also refuses to tackle the disgraceful level of tax imposed upon those who save or invest, as well as those who wish to pass on their assets to their children and grandchildren. And, on top of all these things, it no longer stands up for British interests in what has become an increasingly corrupt, undemocratic and self-serving European gravy train.

Link these things with Mr Cameron's failure to expect higher standards from his ministers, and is it any wonder that people like me are deserting what was once their natural political home?

William Rogers
Kingston upon Thames, Surrey

SIR – Savvy shoppers using Aldi and Lidl forced change on the major supermarkets. Now those who voted UKIP have sent a message to the ruling elite.

Howard Boothroyd
Huddersfield, West Yorkshire

SIR – The UKIP vote is not a wake-up call, but the fire alarm going off.

Dr John Doherty
Stratford-upon-Avon, Warwickshire

SIR – Mainstream parties echo Margaret Thatcher's complaint: 'We are not getting our message out.' They are fooling themselves. They are getting their message out, and we are hearing it, and we just don't like it.

Francis Rutter
Norwich

SIR – David Cameron says he won't lurch. You don't lurch if you don't want to. The nation's up for lurching.

Martin Burgess
Beckenham, Kent

SIR – I take exception to the Conservative Party slogan: 'Vote Farage, get Miliband'. It is reminiscent of the slogan: 'A Liberal vote is a wasted vote'.

Most people who vote for either UKIP or the Liberals do so because they believe in their policies, and are voting from conviction and not for tactical reasons.

Ian Dodsworth
Carnforth, Lancashire

SIR – I am a life-long Tory, and would be happy to wear a badge 'Proud to be a Swivel-eyed Loon'.

I remember Aneurin Bevan calling the Tories vermin; many Tories started wearing the badge 'Vermin'. Bevan was, of course, a socialist, but when the Tory hierarchy starts denigrating its supporters, the time has come to say enough is enough; let's get back to basic Conservatism.

Tony Porter
Southampton

SIR – Your correspondent asks why the Conservatives refer to UKIP members as 'loonies, closet racists and fruitcakes'. The answer is: fear. The Conservative Party is currently in a vacuum between established dogma and new directives.

Interestingly, a similar position faced Robert Peel in 1834, when he revived a declining and discredited Tory Party, damaged beyond repair by Catholic emancipation and political reform.

He asked: 'What will you conserve?' before addressing the key issues of the day, and creating a 'Conservative' party that combined reform with maintaining the cornerstones of the establishment.

To survive, the Conservatives of today need to create a credible future policy structure which 'conserves' what is essential to the country.

Hamish Alldridge
Pittenweem, Fife

SIR – The person who called me and others 'swivel-eyed loons' is obviously unaware that a *loon* is another name for the very handsome Great Northern Diver, a far-sighted

bird that breeds in the far north of Canada but migrates
to our shores for the winter.

Jeremy Brittain-Long
Constantine, Cornwall

SIR — In the words of the Prime Minister, there appear to
be more 'fruitcakes, loonies and closet racists — pretty odd
people' in the constituency of Eastleigh than those prepared to vote for the Left-of-centre party he leads.

Ian Gill
Great Ouseburn, North Yorkshire

SIR — The Tory Party should realize that all swivel-eyed
loons have already decamped to the fruitcake, loony and
closet racist party. It shouldn't worry, as it will have the
support of euro-fanatics, gay married couples and old
Etonians.

A. J. Rogers
Epsom, Surrey

SIR — Ministers have been referring to UKIP members as
clowns. As a writer for the circus magazine the *King Pole*, I
know that, unlike today's politics, the profession of
clowning is an honourable one.

Don Stacey
Great Yarmouth, Norfolk

SIR – Anyone for the Swivel-eyed Loon Party? The public hasn't had much fun in politics since Screaming Lord Such departed.

Derek Sharp
Torquay, Devon

SIR – Your columns have referred to 'Loongate' and 'Swivelgate'. Perhaps there should be a referendum to determine which of these passes into history.

Geoffrey White
Wellow, Somerset

SIR – David Cameron should be careful using bakery analogies. Fruit cake has a very long shelf-life, though that of yesterday's crumpet is very short.

Tim Spencer
Bexhill-on-Sea, East Sussex

SIR – The language of the Lower Fourth seems to prevail these days: *swivel-eyed loons*, *fruitcakes*, *clowns*, *plebs*. At least John Major used medieval Latin to refer to some members of the party as *bastards*.

Linda Read
London SW14

. . . AND WHY I'M NOT

SIR – UKIP is playing one of two games: acting as a pressure group and forcing the Conservative Party to adopt a referendum before 2015, before winding down its electoral presence; or being incredibly sadistic, and wanting to destroy the Tories' hopes of winning against a revived Labour Party because of past betrayals on Europe.

Standing by the railway track playing chicken isn't very responsible when there is a genuine socialist threat on our doorstep.

James A. Paton
Billericay, Essex

SIR – Nigel Farage, the UKIP leader, buys a full-page advertisement to deny that UKIP is a racist party and then, in the same advertisement, peddles the lie that all Romanians are thieves.

Sasha Simic
London N16

SIR – We once contended with the Loony Left. Now the Raving Right confronts us. I'm not sure which I find more alarming.

Richard A. Cook
Southampton

SIR – UKIP councillor David Silvester's comment that the floods are God's wrath at gay marriage legislation brings to mind the serious remark I heard in mid-Wales in the 1970s after we experienced a vigorous earth tremor: 'It's all because of this Sunday football.'

Geoff Neale
Cheltenham, Gloucestershire

SIR – If there is truth behind Councillor Silvester's claims, I would shudder to think what Noah was running away from.

Iain McKie
Totland Bay, Isle of Wight

SIR – UKIP succeeded in the local elections because it said to the voters: 'Whatever it is that you're against, we're against it too.' How many of its new councillors will survive the next election?

Simon Gazeley
Bath, Somerset

SIR – If UKIP continues with its electoral success, we shall be obliged to find another party for our protest votes.

Peter C. Carey
London SW13

SIR – To those who are taken in by Mr Farage I would say: you kip if you wish but I am staying awake.

Uta Thompson
Kew, Surrey

SIR – When I am an old woman, I shall not wear purple – in case people fear I'm a UKIP supporter.

Carol Molloy
Bovey Tracey, Devon

SIR – So Nigel Farage, the leader of UKIP, declines to stand for Patrick Mercer's seat. Of course, there is the danger that he might have won and then he would have had to take politics seriously.

Charles Holden
Lymington, Hampshire

SIR – Is Russell Brand hard of hearing? Whatever he was asked on *Question Time*, he seemed to hear: 'Would you like to shout general abuse at Nigel Farage, mate?'

Martin Burgess
Beckenham, Kent

SIR – When stuck in the car park at Durdle Door recently, I was approached by a Polish lady who kindly offered to push my car out of the mud.

In view of her strength, kindness and courtesy to a stranger, I have reconsidered my support for UKIP and am now in favour of remaining in the European Union.

Hari Bakhshi

Monkston, Buckinghamshire

SIR – We should be grateful that there is a middle-of-the-road party like UKIP, or as in France, many here might have voted for the extreme Right or the extreme Left.

Paul Brazier

Wotton-under-Edge, Gloucestershire

SIR – Did you read about that French performance artist whose act included a dance at a festival with a live rooster attached to his penis? On being convicted of indecent exhibitionism he claimed that the French do not understand art.

It seems to me that they share our views and it will not therefore be necessary to vote for UKIP.

Clive Pilley

Westcliff-on-Sea, Essex

UNBECOMING DEFECTIONS

SIR – Mr Cameron has accused those who defected to UKIP of lying to voters and told them: 'We are coming for you.'

He may find that the electorate feels much the same way about him by next May.

Dick Goodwin
Ware, Hertfordshire

SIR – Mr Cameron appears to have a short memory. Having been elected an MEP for UKIP in 2008, David Campbell Bannerman defected to the Conservative Party in 2011.

He, like Mark Reckless, was elected on the back of supporters 'who stuffed envelopes, who walked streets, who knocked on doors, who worked their guts out'. The difference is that, despite being elected on a party ticket, Mr Campbell Bannerman chose not to do the honourable thing and resign his seat.

Christopher Pratt
Earl Soham, Suffolk

SIR – In 2010 you reported that Mr Reckless was too drunk to vote on the Budget.

Legless and Reckless: he is the perfect candidate for UKIP.

Juliet Henderson
South Warnborough, Hampshire

SIR – I would consider Douglas Carswell's decision more honourable, and less playing to the crowd, if he had to pay the costs of the by-election, instead of it falling on the taxpayers and his constituents.

Duncan Feathers
Bexhill-on-Sea, East Sussex

SIR – In March 1962, as a young reporter, I stood inside the Orpington council chamber some time after midnight and heard the Liberal by-election victor Eric Lubbock cry: 'If we can win here, we can win anywhere!' This might sound familiar to Nigel Farage.

The now Lord Avebury lost the seat in 1970. It has remained Tory ever since.

Peter Willoughby
Tonbridge, Kent

UKIP UNITED F.C.

SIR – At the centre of one of the England flags adorning the house in Rochester, which was immortalized by the tweet by Emily Thornberry, the Labour MP for Islington South and Finsbury, at the by-election, is the logo of West Ham United Football Club.

The Hammers' recent run of success owes much to the recruitment of talented overseas players, which provides a symbolic commentary on UKIP's immigration policies.

Frank Tomlin
Billericay, Essex

SIR – My grandfather was a coal miner and so, by the ordained natural order of things, a Labour supporter; Labour was the party of the working man.

Emily Thornberry's crass tweet shows just how far that party has moved from its roots. What would my grandfather make of the London elite who run it now, with their sneering hostility to the England he knew?

Victor Launert
Matlock Bath, Derbyshire

SIR – Tweeting a picture of a house with flags of St George and a white van is a sackable offence for Labour, but making a key-note conference speech and forgetting to mention the deficit isn't.

Steve Baldock
Handcross, West Sussex

SIR – The last time I pulled up at the traffic lights next to a white van the driver was listening to Allegri's *Miserere*.

Anne Weizmann
Caversham, Berkshire

SIR – I am patriotic, hence I support England teams. I own a white van for the purpose of work, and pay independent school fees for my children.

It now appears that for all three of these activities (and maybe others too) I am despised by the Labour Party. The feeling is mutual.

Dominic Cummings
London SE15

III. Labour Partei.

11. Labour Pains

TWEEDLE-DUM AND TWEEDLE-DUMBER

SIR – To avoid further factional strife and fraternal ill-feeling, why cannot the Milibands take it in turns to be Leader of the Opposition? I doubt that many people outside the Labour Party would notice.

Derek O'Connor
Amersham, Buckinghamshire

SIR – 'Look here, upon this picture, and on this, / The counterfeit presentment of two brothers.'

Soon after, in *Hamlet*, blood was spilt.

Chris James
Llangernyw, Conwy

SIR – Whichever of the Miliband brothers is elected, he will be leader of the Parliamen'ry Par'y in Westmins'er, hoping to be Pry Minis'er.

Robert Perks
London SW19

SIR – With the Blairites and Brownites, I assume Labour now has Milibites.

Peter Fowles
Solihull, West Midlands

SIR – Your report of the prospect of Ed Balls and David Miliband working together as Shadow Chancellor and leader of the Labour Party brought on a severe attack of the TB/GBs in our household.

Martin Hewitt
Ashtead, Surrey

SIR – I listened to Ed Miliband on the *Today* programme yesterday morning. He sounded just like, y'know, Tony Blair with a heavy cold.

Wendy Attridge
Wells, Somerset

SIR – Ed Miliband must be congratulated for winning the leadership contest against the odds.

Perhaps now he is installed, he would like to ponder these chilling statistics. In the last thirty-four years, since the departure of Harold Wilson, Labour has had seven leaders (now including Mr Miliband) but only one of those leaders has actually won a general election.

That one successful Labour leader is Tony Blair, the man the party discarded.

Peter Jackson
Prestbury, Cheshire

SIR — Satisfying as it has been to see the Labour Party shoot itself in the foot, the spectacle of brother pitted against brother has been less enjoyable. I fear Ed Miliband will come to learn, too late, that it is guilt rather than disappointment which is the harder to endure.

Marion Latimer
St Helens, Merseyside

SIR — I would have liked Harriet Harman to be the next Labour leader, so that we could return to the two-party system: the Men Party and the Women Party.

But in her absence, I'll plump for Ed Balls because there is a whiff of craziness about him. I think he will turn out to be a mad megalomaniac; to have him as prime minister would provide endless fun.

Richard Tovey
London SE18

BALLS UP

SIR — I have just listened to a debate on Jeremy Vine's programme. Ed Balls, now Shadow Education Secretary, was discussing what he referred to as 'Skoows' and 'Eyd yoo kayshun'.

For my grandchildren's sake, Coalition, please hang on in there.

Ray Bather
Spartylea, Northumberland

SIR — I would just like to reassure the Prime Minister that he is not alone in finding Ed Balls the most annoying person in modern politics.

Stefan Reynolds
Godalming, Surrey

SIR — If references to the conspiracy to unseat Tony Blair are, according to Ed Balls, 'ancient history', what were Labour's references to the supposedly awful 'Thatcher Years'? Palaeontology?

Russell Hunt
Fleet, Hampshire

SIR — Sometimes it's nice to be told something that you already 'knew', and your revelations about Balls's treachery are the perfect example.

Earl of Ronaldshay
Aske, North Yorkshire

SIR — On a recent trip on Eurostar, my seat was next to that of Ed Balls who, I must admit, I did not recognize at first.

His female colleague offered me the choice of one of their several newspapers, and I asked if she had the *Daily Telegraph*. The reply was that it was the only one they did not have.

I found them both extremely courteous and friendly.

I have to add that we were in the second-class part of the train.

However, it did occur to me that you should always know what your opponents are up to. The best way for the Labour Party to do that is to read the *Daily Telegraph* from cover to cover every day.

George Smith
Canterbury, Kent

SIR – Your columnist Mary Liddell usually makes me so angry that internal bleeding occurs with no need for any help from the aspirin I take. But today she made me laugh out loud twice: once by comparing Mr Miliband to Clement Attlee; the second time by stating that the Labour Party needs Ed Balls to fight and win an election.

How I roared!

S. P.
Headcorn, Kent

SIR – Ed Balls tell us that he 'wants to be himself'. What was he before? A cardboard cut-out? Or just morally and intellectually bankrupt?

Silly little man.

Unfit for any purpose, I would suggest.

David Bird
Esher, Surrey

SIR – Has anyone else drawn a small moustache on a photograph of Ed Balls? Frightening or what!

Stafford Trendall
Overton, Hampshire

SIR – The photograph of Ed Balls's stomach protruding from a football shirt reveals that he might be best advised to undertake a personal programme of quantitative easing.

Juliet Henderson
Warnborough, Hampshire

SIR – Ed Balls has shown great courage performing Schumann in public. The fact that he is also working towards Grade 3 (normally the domain of school-age musicians) shows that his public performance was not just a publicity stunt.

Perhaps George Osborne, the Chancellor, should refrain from poking fun unless he is prepared to show the same courage?

Nick Perry
Lincoln

SIR — You report that *The Antiques Roadshow* and *The Sound of Music* make Ed Balls cry. I'm moved to tears when I recall what he and his cohorts did to this country when they were in power.

Bill Hollowell
Orton Waterville, Cambridgeshire

TALKING ABOUT THEIR GENERATION

SIR — In his first speech as Labour leader in Manchester, Ed Miliband continually stressed that he was of a 'new generation', sounding rather like a Who tribute band.

He then warmly endorsed the London mayoral candidature of Ken Livingstone for 2012, by which time the former leader of the GLC (remember that?) will be sixty-seven years old.

John Axon
Petts Wood, Kent

SIR — Am I alone in hoping that 'his generation' will f-f-fade away?

Peter Wride
Westrip, Gloucestershire

SIR – The more I see and hear Ed Miliband, the more I begin to wonder if he was designed by Matt Pritchett.

Harry Smith
Welwyn Garden City, Hertfordshire

SIR – Ed Miliband must stop starting his interview replies with, 'I guess what I'm saying is . . .' If he has to guess at what his own ideas are, what hope has he of understanding anyone else's?

Revd Philip Foster
Hemingford Abbots, Cambridgeshire

SIR – Tessa Jowell remarks that Ed Miliband is 'discovering his mojo'.

Could someone please enlighten me as to what a 'mojo' is? I think it unlikely that I have one, but it would be good to be sure.

Diana Crook
Seaford, East Sussex

JOYFUL DISUNION

SIR – *Schadenfreude* is generally an unpleasant thing. But when it comes to in-fighting between Labour and Unite, the word is inadequate to describe the joy and hope it gives those who wish neither well.

Charles Foster
Chalfont St Peter, Buckinghamshire

SIR – Before Ed Miliband gets too comfortable on his high horse about donors enjoying secret dinners with David Cameron, it might be worth pointing out that the trade unions do not give the Labour Party funds in order to be ignored.

Ellis Field
York

SIR – Under Labour, donors were accused of paying 'cash for honours'. By cutting out the Lords, the Conservative system of cash for influence looks considerably more efficient.

Tony Manning
Barton on Sea, Hampshire

SIR – Surely Labour Party donors should be entitled to pay £250,000 to excuse themselves from dining with Ed Miliband.

Anthony Rodriguez
Staines, Middlesex

HARD LABOUR

SIR – Ed Miliband has pledged to make the Labour Party 'the party of the grafters'. He's a bit behind the times; three Labour MPs are already in prison for graft.

Ted Hawkins
Sandhurst, Berkshire

SIR – One cannot imagine why prisoners should crave voting rights when we seem to be sending them a regular supply of politicians to share among themselves.

George Langton
Southsea, Hampshire

SIR – It is claimed that a country gets the politicians it deserves. I'm struggling to identify just what it is we have done to be so undeserving.

Michael Hinchliffe
Smeeth, Kent

SIR – In the last few days while watching BBC Parliament, I have observed in the House of Commons chamber: a lady filing her nails, a gentleman yawning repeatedly and a frontbench spokesman apparently chewing. Is this behaviour acceptable, particularly following the expenses scandal?

H. W.
Lesbury, Northumberland

SIR – What most disappointed and outraged me, upon learning of Eric Joyce's brawl in a House of Commons bar, was that it was not shown on the otherwise dreary and tiresome Parliamentary channel.

Nicky Samengo-Turner
Hundon, Suffolk

SIR – I really don't know whether to be more outraged by the behaviour of Eric Joyce MP in the bar at the House of Commons or by the fact that they were holding a karaoke session there. Churchill would be turning in his grave.

David Ellis
Tarves, Aberdeenshire

WHAT THEREFORE THE ELECTORATE HAS JOINED TOGETHER . . .

SIR — I am a firm believer in marriage, but an equally firm believer in sticking to one's principles. The announcement of the Miliband wedding smacks of opportunism, not of affection and commitment.

Even if one accepts that Ed Miliband proposed romantically during a walk on Primrose Hill, one wonders why all the initiative has been portrayed as his, as if 'his long-term partner, Justine' had been waiting with clasped hands and a pious expression for just such a moment.

I would have been far more convinced if they had told the press, after the event, that they had finally married. We could have been pleased for them, and moved on.

Liz Wicken
Royston, Hertfordshire

SIR — Congratulations to Ed and Justine. The best man has been discarded. Again.

John Axon
Petts Wood, Kent

SIR — While I am pleased to see that Edward Miliband is making an honest woman of Justine Thornton, he is still no gentleman. If he were, he would know that he should be on the outside of the pavement in your picture today.

Jonathan L. Kelly
Yatton, Somerset

SIR – Ed Miliband getting married? He'll be pronouncing his 'ts' next.

Charles Vandepeer
Blean, Kent

THIS IS WHAT A SPENDTHRIFT LOOKS LIKE

SIR – I do not know which is worse: the employees who make the 'This is what a feminist looks like' T-shirt being paid 62 pence an hour or Ed Miliband and others, who say there is a cost of living crisis, paying £45 for a T-shirt.

Robin Darby
Birmingham

SIR – Nothing illustrates more precisely why Labour is unfit to govern than Mr Miliband's absurd pronouncement on energy prices. In Canute-like fashion he will hold back market forces, and stop the price of power increasing – presumably supported by state subsidy and government spending. That is how Labour got us into this mess in the run-up to 2010.

Steve Willis
Olney, Buckinghamshire

SIR – Perhaps Mr Miliband would be kind enough to fix the price of oil. As our village in North Oxfordshire has no mains gas, we have to work with the vagaries of the oil market, which seems to be more volatile than the gas or electricity markets.

Failing that, he could always try and fix the price of logs.

David Swan
South Newington, Oxfordshire

SIR – It seems we've moved from the 1992 *Sun* headline: 'If Kinnock wins today, will the last person to leave Britain please turn out the lights', to a possible 2015 one: 'If Miliband wins today, please make your way to the exit as the lights are being turned off'.

Phil Coutie
Twickenham, Middlesex

CONSERVATIVES FOR MILIBAND

SIR – Ed Miliband is having a bit of a wobble, indeed the electorate considers him entirely wobbly, woolly and wonky.

However, thanks to Lib Dem intransigence on boundary reform, our skewed electoral balance might yet make this deeply flawed politician the next prime minister.

My dilemma is whether to ridicule him (a pleasing pastime) or tacitly lend him support, since replacing him with Yvette Cooper or Alan Johnson is tantamount to delivering the keys of No. 10 to the socialists, whereas retaining him offers a fighting chance of Conservative success.

John Axon
Herne Bay, Kent

SIR – To demonize Ed Miliband as a bogeyman is to concede the political initiative. Where is the appeal in the deeply uninspiring 'Vote for us to keep them out'? It is a far cry from the courageous and far-reaching reforms of the Thatcher governments, when the Tory message was positive and clear, rewarded by three general election victories.

David Saunders
Sidmouth, Devon

SIR — Ed Miliband's desire to have four million 'conversations' with voters prior to the election will need them to be short, rather like the last one I had with a Labour canvasser who rang my door bell. I contributed two words, a total of seven letters.

R. Adam
Stevenage, Hertfordshire

JOURNEYING WITH TONY BLAIR

SIR — Thank you for your excellent coverage of Tony Blair's autobiography, *A Journey*. I shall now make my own donation to the Royal British Legion, happy not to have to wade through the entire tome.

Sue Eyles
Maidenhead, Berkshire

SIR — The adjective most commonly used with 'journey' is probably 'wasted'.

David Laycock
Castlemorton, Worcestershire

SIR — If Mr Blair sincerely believes going to war was correct, why on earth does he pledge to devote the rest of his life to making amends?

Paul Kunino
Lynch, Sydney, Australia

SIR – Is a mass book-burning the appropriate response?

David Overend

Yoxall, Staffordshire

SIR – I shall wait for the German edition of *A Journey*. *Eine Fahrt* sounds a much more appropriate title.

Colin Macdonald

Nottingham

SIR – Oh, for heaven's sake, are we supposed to feel sympathy for Tony Blair that Gordon Brown drove him to drink? What did he think the rest of us were doing the entire time he was in power?

Rosanne Greaves

Frodsham, Cheshire

SIR – Is this likely to be one in a series of kick and tell books?

Roger Noons

Kingswinford, West Midlands

SIR – So, Tony Blair found the Queen to be 'haughty', did he? That's how I behave when I can't stand someone.

Christine Phillips

Nottingham

SIR – Perhaps the reason for Tony Blair's absence from the royal wedding was that the Queen couldn't afford his appearance fee.

Paul King
Hassocks, West Sussex

SIR – Tony Blair must have something. He has managed to retain a notional socialism, while becoming the very personification of capitalism.

Pete Taylor
Virginia Water, Surrey

SIR – Tony Blair may have had nine children named after him in Kosovo but on 23 May and 19 June 1818, the Rector of Ilchester baptized no fewer than twenty-six local children, both male and female, Merest Coffin, after the surnames of the two local MPs.

Gerald Masters
Ilchester, Somerset

SIR – The World Cup has bestowed hundreds of names on the newly born. It is a Zulu tradition to name children after events at their birth.

The *Mercury*, a Durban newspaper, published some of the names including: Offside Mchunu, Vuvuzela Mhlongo, Goalkeeper Sitole, Striker Hadabe and Substitute Shandu.

Alan Fairleigh
London SW18

SIR — I can see no point in continuing with the Chilcot Inquiry if Tony Blair is able to block key pieces of evidence. Whatever the outcome of the inquiry, it will be flawed by this omission. It might as well be stopped now and the costs reduced accordingly.

This country has to accept that Tony Blair is too slippery to be caught. Expenses, the Iraq War — there is no paper trail. We need to leave him to his globetrotting and money-raising and move on.

R. M. Ferrie
Mawnan Smith, Cornwall

SIR — Your graphic of Tony Blair's travels over a period of twelve months stopped short of his July 2011 visit to Australia.

Would that he had done the same.

Chris Watson
Carlton River, Tasmania, Australia

12. We Don't Agree
with Nick

THE NEW POLITICS

SIR – Well, that didn't take long, did it ('David Laws resigns over expenses claims', report, 29 May 2010)? Welcome to the sleaze-free new politics.

Jon Hamblin
Hawkhurst, Kent

SIR – While many said that the coalition government would end in tears and, perhaps, cause tears in office, nobody expected it to begin with them.

Francis Purdue-Horan
Bingham, Nottinghamshire

SIR – I thought that Nick Clegg indicated that the expenses scandal was a Labour and Tory problem and that his party was whiter than white.

John Varley
Sidmouth, Devon

I SYMPATHIZE WITH NICK

SIR – I am in the hitherto unlikely position of feeling a little sorry for Nick Clegg. Saddled with David Laws, Vince Cable and Simon Hughes, not to mention ex-colleagues of painful memory such as Mark Oaten, Charles Kennedy, Lembit Öpik and Chris Huhne, he must wonder whether he did something wrong in a previous life.

Tim Hubbard
London SW14

SIR – Do the Liberal Democrats wear sandals because they are easy to kick off in sexual emergencies?

Dr Alan D. Prowse
Leatherhead, Surrey

SIR – Nick Clegg has been much maligned – unfairly in my view. Mr Clegg, through his excellent performance in the television debates, catapulted the Liberal Democrats into power. Those who decry him now – and those who covet his job – should reflect on that. The next general election will almost certainly see the Lib Dems routed at the polls. Mr Clegg will no doubt be blamed, but the real blame will lie with those who created the mess the country is now in. Unpopularity is a certain by-product of recovery for those who make the tough decisions.

Mick Ferrie
Mawnan, Cornwall

SIR – Nick Clegg says he just puts on music and cries. I don't even need the music; I just think of misled politicians ruining our landscape with wind farms.

Celia Hobbs
Penicuik, Midlothian

SIR – Hilaire Belloc anticipated Nick Clegg with his satire on Lord Lundy, who 'was too freely moved to tears'. It must surely be only a matter of time before he is sent to govern New South Wales.

Alasdair Macleod
Newton Poppleford, Devon

PUNISHING HUHNE'S HUBRIS

SIR – Perhaps Chris Huhne should now change his personalized registration plate from H11 HNE to HUBR 1 S.

Nigel Dyson
Ashley, Hampshire

SIR – Given that Chris Huhne and Vicky Pryce have been told to expect a custodial sentence, I suggest they should be made to share a cell in prison. This will give them every opportunity to understand better how they got themselves into this mess in the first place.

Paul Millwood
Welford-on-Avon, Warwickshire

SIR – Perhaps a better sentence for disgraced politicians would be a lifetime ban from public office and media appearances.

Anthony Henderson
Woking, Surrey

SIR – Is it possible that Chris Huhne has persuaded someone to serve his sentence for him? The photograph you published on yesterday's front page scarcely resembles the Chris Huhne before the trial.

John W. Milhofer
Broadstone, Dorset

SIR – My husband is pressuring me to take his Nectar points so that he can have my Avios points. What is a wife to do?

Diane B. Choyce
London W2

SIR – Chris Huhne would do well to be cautious of any advice he receives in the prison's Chelsea-award-winning gardens.

Some years ago, as executive producer, I accepted an invitation to record an edition of BBC Radio 4's *Gardeners' Question Time* at the prison. One inmate asked a very technical question about light levels and day length for maximum plant growth. The team gave a comprehensive answer.

After the recording, a prison officer took me to one side and explained that the inmate who posed the question was serving time for growing cannabis on an industrial scale, and we had just given him chapter and verse on increasing his crop yield. I decided not to include that question in the broadcast programme.

Trevor Taylor

Chipping Norton, Oxfordshire

SIR – Chris Huhne has been released from prison having only served eight weeks of an eight-month sentence.

I was sent to a minor public school where I had to endure damp, cold dormitories, horrid food, tepid showers, regular cross-country runs and teachers who I felt had failed elsewhere in life.

This regime lasted for five long years.

David Turton

Heathfield, East Sussex

'ME TIME' FOR THE DEPUTY PRIME MINISTER

SIR – When Margaret Thatcher was Prime Minister, she was known to ring ministers and senior civil servants at three o'clock in the morning, seeking an explanation of some paper they had buried in her red boxes. How times change.

I advise David Cameron not to go on holiday during

the present crises in the Middle East, as his deputy might be enjoying 'me time' instead of keeping abreast of developments.

Michael Bacon
Farnham, Surrey

SIR – I think it a little unfair to berate Nick Clegg for forgetting he was running the country in the Prime Minister's absence; after all, everyone else did.

Derrick Pepperell
Cheltenham, Gloucestershire

SIR – Nick Clegg's plan not to accept more papers after 3 p.m. is nothing new. Field Marshal Viscount Slim – perhaps one of our most successful field commanders, who was responsible for the defeat of Japan in Burma – would finish at 3 p.m. He would then read a novel for an hour or so and then go for a walk, eat at 7.30 p.m. and be in bed by 10 p.m.

He felt that generals who rushed around wore themselves and their subordinates out, so that when a real emergency developed nobody had the reserves of vigour to enable them to work day and night if need be.

Nick Clegg's decision, therefore, is to be commended.

Dr James Cave
Newbury, Berkshire

CABLE CAR CRASH

SIR — In your leading article, you say that it is time for Vince Cable, the Business Secretary, to move on.

I have an idea — he should form his own company, and try to run it under the current tax and regulatory regime.

Frank Maycock

Gatehouse of Fleet, Dumfries and Galloway

SIR — Clement Attlee is reputed to have once told Harold Laski, then the Labour Party chairman, that 'a period of silence from you would be welcome'.

David Cameron can't be the only one who feels the same about Vince Cable.

Roger Pierce

Chinnor, Oxfordshire

SIR — Don't overestimate Vince Cable. His only real political ambition has been to get a railway carriage to himself.

Malcolm Parkin

Kinnesswood, Kinross

SIR — Why, in 2007, was Menzies Campbell (born in 1941) considered to be too old to lead the Liberal Democrats; while, in 2014, Vince Cable (born in 1943) is being touted as successor to Nick Clegg?

Alec Ellis
Liverpool

SIR — May we assume that the only reason Vince Cable remains in the Cabinet is that David Laws is not yet in a position to take his place?

Richard Coulson
Maidstone, Kent

VERY ALTERNATIVE VOTING

SIR — I noticed that there were only two options on the AV ballot paper: Yes or No. What happened to 'Good God, No'?

Ralph Griffiths
New Malden, Surrey

SIR — I find it difficult enough to pick one candidate in an election, let alone three.

N. P. Scott
Harpenden, Hertfordshire

SIR – I voted 1 for No and 2 for Yes just to prove I under-
stood the system.

Alan E. Quaife
Loughton, Essex

SIR – The Electoral Commission can explain first past
the post in fifty-nine words but needs 351 words to
explain AV. Having attended the count for two constituencies at the last general election, I was amazed at how
many of my fellow citizens struggled with the concept of
putting a single X in the box. As well as the X, we had
ticks, lines and circles, some of which were placed immediately next to the candidate's name or in the margin of
the voting form. I shudder to think how such voters
would cope with AV.

Guy Griffiths
Leominster, Herefordshire

SIR – Only three countries use the Alternative Vote
system: Australia, Fiji and Papua New Guinea. Of those,
Fiji is currently trying to get rid of it, and in Australia, the
system is so unpopular that voting has had to be made
compulsory. Why is it even being considered for us?

Paul Wilson
Little Canfield, Essex

SIR – I sampled the AV referendum debate through satellite television, hoping that it would equal the passion of Britain's Reform Bill crisis of 1831–2, and emulate the cogency of New Zealand's national seminar on voting reform in 1992–3.

Alas, all I caught was an advertisement for the Yes campaign which showed how AV could help ten insipid young people decide whether to go to a pub or a coffee bar. Surely they could have found a pub that served coffee?

Professor Ged Martin
Youghal, County Cork, Ireland

SIR – If Nick Clegg can share the reins of power under the present voting system, it is not a change to the system we need, but an alternative to democracy.

Andrew Courtney
Hampton Wick, Middlesex

CHECKS AND BALANCES

SIR – I had not realized that I was in favour of keeping the Lords as it is until Nick Clegg suggested changing it.

Richard Jenkins
Long Compton, Warwickshire

SIR – Lord Hennessy of Nympsfield has put his finger on it. The House of Lords should consist of people who know rather than believe things.

Treleven Haysom
Langton Matravers, Dorset

SIR – Perhaps it is wise to take note of W. S. Gilbert's words in *Iolanthe* (1882) about the House of Lords, that they: 'did nothing in particular, and did it very well'. Maybe, then, just leave things as they are.

Bernard Lockett
Folkestone, Kent

SIR – After failing with the Alternative Vote and reform of the House of Lords, Nick Clegg's call to disestablish the Church of England will be welcome news for those who support the status quo.

Malcolm Watson
Welford, Berkshire

SIR – I am grateful to David Cameron for rejecting Nick Clegg's call. His embracing of antidisestablishmentarianism has allowed me to achieve my long-held ambition to use this word in context.

Dr S. V. Steinberg
Prestwich, Lancashire

SIR — Seemingly forgetting his oath as a privy counsellor in his fifth-form debating society attack on 500 years of constitutional settlement is par for Mr Clegg's course.

Loving England much, but Europe more, he demonstrates the truth of Elizabeth I's dictum: 'Who hath two strings to one bow may shoot strong but never straight.'

Robert Stephenson
Henley-on-Thames, Oxfordshire

WAGGING THE TAIL OF THE COALITION DOG

SIR — How come Mr Cameron and co are looking to water down policies to mollify the Lib Dems when, if there was a general election tomorrow, the Lib Dems would be returned to the size of party that, once again, could hold its meetings in a phone box — if they could find one?

Geoff Eley
Dunmow, Essex

SIR — I am confused. The Lib Dems take a drubbing at the polls, but then their politicians respond by saying that this means they must impose their will more firmly on coalition policy.

Earl of Balfour
London SW3

SIR – An advantage in having the Lib Dems in the coalition is that it is easier to see the idiotic ideas of Vince Cable and Danny Alexander and the incompetence of Nick Clegg. There is no clearer indication why a vote for that party is lunacy.

Clifford Baxter

Warlingham Surrey

SIR – The Liberal Democrats should realize that 'everyone else is wrong' is not a political philosophy; it is a clear sign of immaturity.

Just ask any teacher who has to deal with disruptive teenagers.

Brian Christley

Abergele, Denbighshire

SIR – There is nothing remarkable about the willingness of Liberal Democrat ministers to make disparaging comments about their Conservative coalition colleagues. They are following the example of Lloyd George, the last Liberal prime minister.

During his coalition government of 1916–22 he ridiculed his foreign secretary, Arthur Balfour, as 'the scent on a pocket handkerchief'. He castigated his closest Tory colleague, Bonar Law, as 'weak', adding 'B. L. ought to take to drink' to give himself courage.

Curzon was 'insufferably pompous'. Salisbury, head of the great Tory house of Cecil, 'would make a very respectable booking clerk'. Colleagues rushed to deliver the insults to their victims.

Lloyd George had the great merit of never minding what other people said about him. He paid heed to some wise words of Anthony Trollope; 'It is a common practice for people to make disobliging observations about one another. Why do we profess such shock and surprise when we hear what is being said about us?'

Alistair Cooke
London SW1

THE LAST WORD ON THE COALITION

SIR – I have never found a collective noun for clowns. If there isn't one, may I humbly suggest a *coalition*?

Peter Pascall
Worsley, Lancashire

SIR – As a Conservative branch chairman, I read your report 'Cameron plans for a second coalition' with interest. So is his rallying cry now, to us poor foot soldiers: 'Go back to your constituencies and prepare for defeat'?

Mark Hudson
Smarden, Kent

SIR — I suggest David Cameron also seeks a coalition with Labour, and we can stop wasting money on elections.

Brian Gilbert

Hampton, Middlesex

SIR — Am I alone in thinking that Gordon Brown, Alistair Darling *et al.* seem far less incompetent in retrospect?

Bruce Chalmers

Goring-by-Sea, West Sussex